Medieval Secular Literature

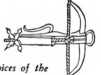

Published under the auspices of the
CENTER FOR MEDIEVAL AND RENAISSANCE STUDIES
University of California, Los Angeles

Contributions of the
UCLA CENTER FOR MEDIEVAL AND RENAISSANCE STUDIES
1: Medieval Secular Literature: Four Essays

UCLA CENTER FOR
MEDIEVAL AND RENAISSANCE STUDIES
CONTRIBUTIONS: I

Medieval
Secular Literature

Four Essays

Edited by
WILLIAM MATTHEWS

UNIVERSITY OF CALIFORNIA PRESS
BERKELEY AND LOS ANGELES, 1967

University of California Press
Berkeley and Los Angeles, California
Cambridge University Press
London, England

THE CONTRIBUTORS

WILLIAM MATTHEWS, Professor of English at the University of California, Los Angeles, since 1939, has published on the history of the pronunciation of English and its dialects, on Cockney, on American history, on British and American diaries and autobiographies, and especially on late medieval literature, notably the Arthurian. He will shortly issue a new biographical study of Sir Thomas Malory and a definitive edition of Pepys's diary.

PHILLIP W. DAMON, Professor of English at the University of California, Santa Barbara, is equally concerned with both Greco-Roman and medieval literature; he had previously taught English at Cornell, and Classics at Harpur College and Ohio State University. He has published a monograph with William C. Helmbold on Propertius, and the book *Modes of Analogy in Ancient and Medieval Verse*.

URBAN TIGNER HOLMES, JR., Kenan Professor of Romance Philology at the University of North Carolina, where he has taught since 1925, plays a preeminent role in the effort to understand medieval literature through the archaeological and numismatic, as well as the written, remains of the time that produced a particular work. His *Daily Living in the Twelfth Century* admirably reflects this wide view.

STEPHEN G. NICHOLS, JR., formerly Assistant Professor of French at the University of California, Los Angeles, currently in the Department of Comparative Literature, University of Wisconsin, is particularly concerned with medieval epics and histories. In 1961 he published *Formulaic Diction and Thematic Composition in the Chanson de Roland*.

PREFACE

On the weekend of April 17–18, 1964, the Center for Medieval and Renaissance Studies at the University of California, Los Angeles, held the first of what it intends to be an enjoyable and profitable series of colloquia on medieval and Renaissance subjects of many kinds. This first gathering was devoted to medieval secular literature. The participants, numbering sixty-five, were members of the Los Angeles Center and thirty of their guests—kindred spirits from Harvard University, the University of North Carolina, and the Berkeley, Santa Barbara, Riverside, and Davis campuses of the University of California.

A Welsh parson, so it is reported, once explained the homiletic tradition as having two methods. The one favored by most of Christendom, he declared, was for the preacher to convey his teaching in logical sequence, to address the congregation with points numbered, as it were, Roman one, Roman two, and so on, until he delighted his eager audience with a conclusion that was the capstone of unity. In Welsh Wales, on the other hand, the preacher's method was simply to touch on a variety of significant things, not many of them connected. In this way, or so he hoped, his sermon would inevitably contain something to capture the imagination or the mind of each of his parishioners and start him on a train of personal meditation. The success of any Welsh sermon could therefore be easily judged. If anyone was still listening at the end, it was a failure.

The intents of the committee that arranged this first

meeting were in a sort Cambrian. The company was to be mixed; not medieval literary specialists alone, but also experts on medieval and Renaissance art, history, music, science, and other subjects, too. The occasion was intended to be one of delight as well as teaching. So the committee simply invited the main speakers to say something that they really wanted to say, but hinted that they say it in a way suited to the company and the occasion.

The essays that follow suggest the nature of the gathering and some of its spirit. They reflect the variety of topics, moods, and approaches with which the speakers responded to the committee's suggestions. Lacking, alas, is anything to represent the lengthy, animated, and highly informed discussion that followed each paper, or the gay conversation on medieval and modern concerns which welded the whole.

The Center rejoices in the social and scholarly success of this the first of its series, and wishes to thank all those who contributed to its intellectual conviviality. It offers this little book to colleagues elsewhere in the hope that it will give a still wider pleasure and stimulus.

WILLIAM MATTHEWS
Chairman of the Conference Committee

CONTENTS

INHERITED IMPEDIMENTS IN MEDIEVAL LITERARY HISTORY

William Matthews

ANY YEARS AGO, as an innocent young Englishman who was curious about matters American, I stumbled on things that rather astonished me. In collaboration with the late Dixon Wecter, I was compiling a book about ordinary Americans and their wars. I had never studied American history formally, so for a compass for my own half of the book, I was dependent upon scholarly studies—histories, biographies, and so on. They served their turn so nobly that the book outran the outrage that might have been expected to crush so alien and amateur an invasion of the local Tom Tiddler's ground. But at some points they proved the most broken of reeds. With the American Loyalists, for example. To me, some of these people, men like Governor Thomas Hutchinson, intelligent, sensitive, torn several ways, tragic in their experience, were fascinating. Having read their own records, I assumed that simple interest in a good human story must have led scores of scholars toward them long since. In fact, apart from Kenneth Roberts' novel and a journalist's book called *Divided Loyalties,* I could find almost nothing about them. This dearth of biographies and overall studies was not to be explained by lack of materials—the libraries were stuffed with their letters and diaries—and the only explanation I could imagine was that an inherited and prob-

ably unconscious partisanship had so affected the writing
and teaching of American history that it had induced
blindness to subjects whose attractions would otherwise
have been inescapable. I should perhaps add that the chapter I wrote about them does not appear in the book: we
had too much material, it was wartime, and we and the
publishers came to an unargued agreement that Loyalists
were, as the term then went, "expendable."

Neglects of this kind are not restricted to Americans,
and they are not unknown in studies of remoter ages. Nor,
indeed, are they peculiar to recent scholars; the Middle
Ages notoriously neglected much of the classical literature
that it also preserved. And this medieval neglect cannot be
attributed solely to the disorder that attended Alaric and
the later barbarian breeds; much of it, surely, must have
stemmed from those Christian preconceptions that are represented in the writings of Orosius and St. Augustine.
Generally splendid as Antiquity may seem to us, to Chris-
tians of the fifth century—although they too admired
some things—the essence of the classical past was a devil's
brew of superstition, corruption and violence.

So common are these neglects, in fact, so peculiar and
human their explanations, that at the time I was surprised
by the American instance I was reminded of an astonish-
ment of a decade before, when I first read R. W. Chambers'
On the Continuity of English Prose. The argument of that
luminous and exciting discussion is that the tradition of
English devotional prose was unbroken from the tenth
century to the sixteenth. In developing this thesis, Chambers was urged by two inspirations: his love match with
Sir Thomas More, and a sudden necessity to fend off an
attack upon medieval literary studies; a very short time before the essay appeared, a royal commission had recom-
mended that the teaching of English literature might more
profitably be begun with Chaucer than with Anglo-Saxon

writings. Chambers' thesis is now suffering from its defensive inspiration; critics have been suggesting that it finds continuities where none may exist and that it pays no attention to the continental sources of English mysticism. Nevertheless, the essay continues to be a mainspring of literary scholarship in England. And that is because it drew attention to a great body of distinguished devotional prose that had been almost forgotten. Not forgotten entirely, of course: the *Cambridge History of English Literature* finds room in its fourteen large volumes to give one page to the *Ancrene Riwle*, a page to Walter Hilton, a short paragraph to Julian of Norwich, and almost four pages to Richard Rolle—though most of those four pages are taken up with Rolle's verse, including the *Prick of Conscience* which he certainly did not write. But there is no mention at all of Nicholas Love, *The Cloud of Unknowing*, Dionysius' *Hid Divinitie*, the life of Marjorie Kempe, *The Revelations of St. Brigid*, *The Chastising of God's Children*, and all the other fine, substantial devotional treatises that have recently been claiming editorial attention.

This grudgingness in the great *Cambridge History* does not reflect any indifference to religious writing as such, for its four pages on Rolle are immediately followed by twenty on Wycliffe, and its brief notes on Hilton and Julian come as an appendix to a lengthy discussion of the Lollards and Reginald Pecock. Nor is it to be explained by inaccessibility; manuscripts of this material are abundant, and German and French studies had long since stressed its merit and importance. The disproportion in the *Cambridge History* must reflect the editors' and writers' sense of relative values. But those values cannot be ordinary ones, since the literary quality of the slighted works and their contemporary popularity and importance are in no way inferior to those of Wycliffe and certainly not of Pecock. What *may* explain the proportions is that while Wycliffe is held to have anticipated the Reformation, and Pecock is concerned with reformist Lollardry, the neglected writers are eremitical contemplatives firm in the orthodoxies of monastic Catholicism. Something of the kind may also explain the great attention that is paid to the painful Purvey translation of the Bible and the little attention that goes to the rather elegant partial translations that come from more orthodox quarters. If this is indeed the explanation, then the mystics were in the same boat as the American Loyalists; people who prove to have got on the wrong side in a national issue may have to wait an extremely long time before they get the historical attention that their activities might suggest. Had it not been for Chambers' own religious development and his growing absorption in the saintly Sir Thomas More, the English mystics might be waiting still.

Let me cite one further example, a minuscule one this time. Three or four years ago, while I was working on medieval biography and autobiography, I chanced upon something which was considerably out of my line and my competence, but which intrigued me. It was a fifteenth-century book about an eminent English statesman who worked for Henry V and Henry VI. I had been drawn to it by a reference that suggested it was a biography in English, and had it been so, it would have been the earliest surviving example. In fact, there proved to be little writing at all in the book. The manuscript consisted of fifty-two full-page pictures, lively though rather unpolished line drawings, which set out the subject's life and adventures from birth to burial. The writing consisted simply of brief legends to the drawings. A little poking around turned up three rather similar things of about the same time and place. The manuscripts were mentioned briefly in the standard art histories for the period, there were a few articles about them in the *Burlington Magazine* and elsewhere, and one of the manuscripts had been published once in the eighteenth century and twice since. But nowhere could I find any discussion of what intrigued me. In medieval literature there are religious biographies almost without end; but truly secular biographies, especially in the vernaculars, are pretty rare. In painting, I knew things like Giotto's biographical series on Christ and St. Francis; I also knew the copious illustrations in such books as the *Life of St. Louis*. But all these are religious or essentially religious subjects, and in manuscripts the pictures are ancillary to the writing. For all their lack of distinction as art, therefore, these picture books about fifteenth-century secular Englishmen seemed to me to be very interesting in their subject and in their form, and for my own literary purposes, I was eager to learn whether there were other things of the kind. So, since the art histories said nothing about picture biographies, I turned to art historians. (Before I report my experience, I should say that I am considerably indebted to historians of medieval art and that I also feel a humble admiration for them—their concern with the fine detail of craftsmanship leads them toward certainties that the literary historian can only envy, and it is a concern that literary historians might do well to imitate.) The first expert I asked declared, flatly and finally, that there was not and could not have been any such thing in the Middle Ages. The second was intrigued, but regretted that this period was too late for him. The third was so impressed by the unique originality of the concept that he declared the artist must have been Italian, or at any rate Dutch. The fourth knew no exact parallel, but suggested a variety of analogues, particularly the tournament books, which might have provided a suggestion for this highly original device. I returned, therefore, better provided than I went. I was pretty well assured that medieval picture biographies of seculars were even rarer than literary ones, and that the artist who did these jobs had an original mind even if he was not a particularly good draftsman.

But what impressed me most during these bookish and personal inquiries was the evidence that even art historians have their own varieties of the preconceptions that, in rare moments of grace, I sometimes recognize in myself as a literary historian. In the course of considering the self-portraits of medieval writers, I had already been forced to question the dogma that medieval painters and sculptors never drew portraits or self-portraits, that such a concern with the individual was a Renaissance trait *tout simple,* and that medieval artists were on all occasions absorbed by conventional typology. Now, I was forced to question period-identifying assumptions about England and originality. The *facts* in the matter are that all the manuscripts came from Warwickshire and that they were all done during the later fifteenth century. There is no evidence whatsoever that they were not done by an Englishman; most likely, they are in some way related to the local cult of Guy of Warwick and to the work of the native builders and sculptors who created the remarkable Beauchamp chapel at St. Mary's in Warwick.

Observations of this sort over the years have persuaded me, in a general way, that many obvious things in history, big things and little things, fail to get the attention they may deserve simply because some unexamined traditional idea or attitude gets in the way. Similarly, I think, some things in history are usually interpreted or evaluated in ways that might not seem the most patent to people who do not share the determining ideas and attitudes. What I propose to do in the rest of this talk is to throw out some quite blatant generalizations about some of these inherited impediments in medieval literary history, and to salt them with a scattering of examples.

Among the most effective impediments, it seems to me, is what might be called a residuum from the concept of The Renaissance. I don't mean to flog a horse that has so long been refusing to die. Only undergraduates, and people at large, now believe completely in these absolutes or think that "medieval!" is a precise insult as well as a just one. Moreover, since the Fall of the Roman Empire is also coming under scholarly attack, and since it is doubtful that Modern Times can go on forever, it is not altogether impossible that some day the whole notion of medievalism may disappear. Habit, however, vested interest, convenience, and the ancient human love for simple triads, are likely to prevail for a long time to come. And so, "Middle Ages" will continue, despite our better knowledge, to remain a singular noun.* And while it does so, I believe we may continue to think of medieval literature in ways that the pattern promotes—to think of it, for example, generally rather than individually, as though it were a product of time or tradition rather than of men. The anonymity of so much medieval writing contributes to this generalization, of course; when a work can be referred to only by title, and even that title may be an editor's convenience, it is not easy to think that it was not written by Zeit Geist, the same remarkable fellow, all soul and hands, no face, who also built all those Gothic cathedrals.

Medieval anonymity and our own cyclic thinking combine to produce peculiarities in the usual history of medieval literature. All literary histories necessarily employ patterns and generalizations; but the patterns that are favored for more recent times—fashions, coteries, revolts, new ideas—are framed to the recognition of individual enthusiasms and achievements. Histories of medieval liter-

* The plural form in English is presumably meant to avoid semantic confusion. It is pleasant to think that a quirk of linguistics should provide a hole in the fence through which English-speaking scholars could, if they would, crawl into greater freedom.

ature, however, are characteristically organized by literary types. The historian will describe the inherited *matière* and the organizational traits of a certain genre, and then go on to record the major exemplars and the more obvious variations in form during his whole period, from the inception to the decline. Having done this, he then turns to another genre and goes through the same process. This typological method, which inevitably stresses the common themes and the general characteristics, is apt to make the individual author a passenger in history rather then a driver. Inevitably, too, it favors beginnings, and even what precedes beginnings, over the necessarily less striking innovations of what follows. Reports on the medieval literary genres customarily start with a cheer and end on a whimper. The method is not without its conveniences; and it is certainly not without its justifications. But it is a cyclic approach, and a disjointed one, nothing to satisfy a historian who believes that in the Middle Ages, as in other times, books were products of individual men reacting to their own natures and materials and to the manifold ideas, activities, and personages of their own particular days. Were any student, for example, to become interested in learning what was the medieval literary scene at any particular time—that is, what books were being written, what was fusty or fashionable, what subjects or ideas or techniques were coming in or going out, who the new men were and who the old guard, who were paying the piper, where the Bloomsburys were—he would not find the histories the handiest sources of information. By bringing together the openings of the sections on the various genres he might be able to assemble an unstructured mosaic for the decades around 1200; for fifty years later he would have fewer and smaller pieces; after 1300 he would find fragments indeed.

"Literary scene," of course, means something very different for 1260, say, than for 1960. Our own social and technical arrangements ensure that it applies to something more tightly knit than it could have done earlier. But every medieval man was a modern man: the present, and what of the past was valid for the present, was his realm of knowledge and interest. Teaching in the minstrel schools and the schools of rhetoric may have been somewhat traditional— that is always the way with academies—but it would have been a strange writer indeed, however medieval, who could have been indifferent to the subjects, the ideas, the techniques of his successful contemporaries, not only in his own line but in others besides. One has only to imagine oneself in his shoes to raise unending questions about the interrelationships of literary contemporaries. Such questions about the manifold patterns of a literary world living in a present time are questions proper for literary history. But our curious student will find little about them in works that are arranged in diachronic genre patterns. This arrangement, verticals and almost no horizontals, may be excused by the paucity of our knowledge about contemporary relationships. But may not that very paucity have the same explanation as the patterns themselves? Our inherited habit is to think of *le moyen âge* as something all of a piece.

Nor, were the same inquisitive student to become curious about the variety of literary talent and personality among medieval writers, would he be likely to find anything but the most fitful information. Thanks to Menendez Pidal, he would probably learn that the anonymous authors of *The Cid* were men of highly individual tastes and judgments. He would gather as much about a few great-name writers, particularly the earlier of them. He might even be led to suspect something of the kind about the nameless poets who wrote *Beowulf* and the *Roland,* even though their individual geniuses are now being obliterated under a deep snow of papers on their traditional oral formulas. And he would guess that individual personalities explain the unconventionalities of an *Aucassin and Nicolette,* a *Sir Orfeo,* or a *Vision of MacConglinne.* But for the vast majority, for all the known and unknown authors of lesser works, he would get no such impression. For it is our inherited habit to think generally and impersonally about the bulk of medieval writing. In evidence, let me cite a statement by a man I admire, but this side of idolatry: "Chaucer's whole literary career shows him emerging from the average opinion and manner of his contemporaries, and coming out from the medieval crowd to stand apart by himself, individual and free." That is W. P. Ker, Chambers' teacher and one of the most sensitive and knowledgeable of all critics of medieval literature. Elsewhere, Ker may occasionally be seen embracing some minor work which no one else loves. But even his instinct is the same as that of lesser historians: to set his few Gullivers in Lilliput. Yet, as we all know, Lilliputians become human if only one peers close enough. Consider, for example, the donnish delights of the man who mimicked Ovid and then fathered the *Pamphilus* upon him; consider what fascination with horror made the tender Gregory of Tours depict a psychotic world around him; consider the Bourgeois de Paris, surely the wisest and most unusual average sensual Frenchman who ever put pen to vellum; or John Gower, that genteel and elegant victim of his own social conscience; or Sir John Mandeville, so like Pepys, so delightful in his clutching curiosity, ever with child to see some new thing; or Eustache Deschamps, explosive, sardonic, jovial, sentimental by turns; or the unknown author of *The Cloud of Unknowing,* an intellectual, a mystic, and a most gentlemanly man; or Thomas Usk, that mincing mimic of his betters; or Hrotswitha, that up-to-date, solemn-comic female educator; or Guillaume de Deguileville, severest of Cistercians, but one who secretly harbored the romance of a St. Brendan. Consider, too, poor Thomas Occleve, the saddest, nicest, most ink-stained little madman in all English letters. It would be only too easy to go on *ad nauseam;* one may think what one will of their quality as writers, but the literary personalities of this crowd, the lesser medieval authors, are as richly diverse as those of any other period. Even the collections of exemplary stories reveal, in their selection, arrangement, proportions, emphases, and style, the minds and tastes of the compilers. Petrus Alfonsi, Jacques de Vitry, Manning of Brunne, Caesar of Heisterbach, Gautier de Coincy, Geoffroi de la Tour Landry, Arnold of Liège, may share a moral purpose and a moral method, but their compilations reveal them as different people, and so do even the anonymous collections. It is only our obsession with the genres, the traditions, the common matter, the *topoi,* the conventions, The Medieval Mind, which blunts our sense of medieval individualities, of the *discordia concors,* which, being human, is as medieval as it is modern.

It is the lesser writers who suffer most. But our predisposition to an overall view not infrequently affects discussion of even those obviously great writers in whom we must recognize individuality. Thus, we tend to speak of *amour courtois, amour paramours,* in medieval literature as if the term represented a single concept, a single attitude, ignoring the variety of behavior and the many viewpoints that are plain to see in, and even within, Thomas, Béroul, William of Aquitaine, Chrétien de Troyes, Jean de Meun, Gottfried, Ulrich von Lichtenstein, Chaucer, Machaut, Boccaccio, Malory, to list but a few. Similarly, it is our habit to speak of medieval tragedy as though there were a single concept and a single form, as if we had never noticed any difference at all between the *De casibus virorum* and *Roland, Raoul de Cambrai, Tristan, Njals saga, La Mort Artu, Troilus and Criseyde,* or the *Morte Arthure.*

Religion, however, is the area where generalization about the Middle Ages is most general. Most scholars, doubtless, would hedge a great deal if they were called on to justify characterizing a thousand years as an "Age of Faith," though that is a not infrequent title for the Middle Ages, one that is used to allay resentment against it. Books on heresies are numerous, and there is at least one on medieval skepticism—I wish there were also a book on medieval weekday indifference. But in literary matters, the ancient habit of generalizing about medieval religion leads logically to such works as D. W. Robertson's recent book on medieval aesthetics, with its assumptions that medieval writers and their audiences were all expert in Christian exegesis, that the medieval worldview was consistently hierarchical, that almost every item in medieval poetry and narrative—fabliaux and romances as well as the *Divine Comedy* and *Piers Plowman*—is an allegory in praise of the Creator and his world or in condemnation of the Devil and his. Robertson is excessive, many of us think, but he is not alone. To judge from a long string of articles during the past few years, there will soon not remain a single Old English poem that has not been interpreted as an allegory of the spiritual pilgrim. One does not question the extent of medieval piety in doubting the validity of so wholesale an approach. Even the saints, one suspects, were not always sanctimonious.

What seems apparent from all this is that, even though we may question the validity of triading history, we may still continue in the generalizing habits that the triad pattern induces. And this legacy, I think, may also be the explanation for various judgments and neglects that might be thought somewhat regrettable.

"Renaissance" is a biological metaphor, and it implies a cyclic theory of history: that a new culture is born as an old culture dies. In the broadest triad, the Fall of the Roman Empire is complemented by the Renaissance that began a thousand years later. By a process of border-raiding, however, medieval scholars have contrived to redeem the Middle Ages from this notion of a *nuit gothique* antarctic in duration; we now have our own renaissances, several of them. But someone must pay the price of a metaphor. If the eighth, twelfth, and thirteenth centuries, and in England the tenth and the fourteenth, are to bask in the regard that we reserve for a renaissance, other centuries must needs play the role of Déclin, Untergang, Degeneration, and suffer the resultant contempt or neglect. Thus it happens that histories of medieval literature shut up shop at hours that might seem premature. Italian literary history is complex in this matter: its late Middle Ages and its early Renaissance so overlap that in their contention almost every major writer of the *Trecento* suffers a Solomon's Judgment. But the history of medieval French literature characteristically stops about 1300 and so does the German, and the Latin literary history stops rather earlier. The English typically ends as late as 1400; but then, for a reason to which I shall turn soon, its high tide is made to come later than the others. Even when the histories go further, commonly because a section or a volume on the Renaissance is to follow, the writers of the Decline get very short shrift. One would not easily guess from the brief accounts of Guillaume de Machaut, for example, that he was so prolific, inventive, and admirable a writer as men thought him for nearly two centuries. Rather, he is sacrificed to our concept of fourteenth-century degeneration. The ease, the wit, the elegance that his contemporaries recognized in him, the technical virtuosity and inventiveness that they admired and tried to imitate are all regarded by the historian as form without inspiration, sound signifying nothing, a hollow echo of the *Roman de la rose,* something for a historian's perfunctory scorn. Nor would the student suspect from the usual history that other French writers of that time were so lively and individualistic as they actually are, or that there was a great deal of interest in romance during the period and not a little narrative experiment with it. And were it not for the piety of Henri Champion and his disciples, the fifteenth-century French and Burgundian writers would seem even more neglected; apart from some sixteenth-century prints, we do not even have editions of some of their major writings.

But let me turn to England. For the long period, about 140 years, between Chaucer's death and the blessed relief of Wyatt and Surrey, the normal historical picture is almost a Waste Land. Apart from Fortescue, Pecock, Henryson, and Malory—Skelton and Dunbar seem to live in enclaves of their own—the historian sees hardly an original idea or literary device in the whole period, hardly a work worth reading. Literature, he declares, is given over to incompetent imitation, the *danse macabre* fills men's minds, the poets are hacks who lack even a sense of rhythm. Had the historians been paid to do so, I doubt that they could have been more successful in dissuading everybody from reading Lydgate, Occleve, and their successors. Generally, this literary portrait is matched to a desolated landscape of social decadence, a world in which even the supposed author of *Le Morte Darthur* could rob and rape and not be counted a villain. But without denying the Wars of the Roses or the weakness of Henry VI, it may still be questioned whether the English fifteenth century was quite so blasted a heath. In music, Dunstable's disciples and the Eton School cut no mean figure; from Richard Beauchamp and Dick Whittington to Margaret of York, the roll-call of literary patrons makes a quite splendid sound; Duke Humphrey is only the best known of bibliophiles in the grand style; Eton and King's show a reasonably serious concern with education, as well as some architectural talent; the magnificent portrait figure that William Austen carved for the tomb of Richard Beauchamp has been compared with Donatello's work, and that of Bishop Beckington at Wells is scarcely less splendid; my little Warwickshire artist had novel ideas at least; great "wool churches" like Fairford and Lavenham are remarkable for their abundance as well as their beauty; King's College chapel, St. George's at Windsor, and Henry VII's at Westminster have their own magnificence; fortified manors, Herstmonceux Castle, and Hever appeal wondrously to the eye, even if military historians do protest that their walls are degenerately thin and that they pay too much heed to comfort; Burford and Broadway and Laycock are still the most pleasing of small English towns. In fact, were one to abstract from the English scene all its legacy from the fifteenth century, an extraordinarily large part of its beauty would be gone. Chaos, a chaos that preceded the Tudor Renaissance, is clearly not the whole story, or so one would judge by fifteenth-century things still delightfully audible and visible.

Nor is the literary achievement of the period quite so meagre as historians have made it. For the literary historian, the fourteenth century is our medieval renaissance, and his witnesses are not only Chaucer, Gower, Langland, and the Gawain poet, but also a large number of substantial poems, several of them heroic in character. But the manuscripts of many of these poems are fifteenth-century work, some of them late fifteenth-century; and many years ago W. W. Skeat voiced his suspicions that some of them, particularly some of the long narrative poems that are conventionally credited to the fourteenth-century alliterative revival, may have been composed during the fifteenth century. His caveat remains valid, unregarded though it has been; and it is possible to suggest still further examples—*Life and Death*, for instance, a poem of quite remarkable power and brilliance, written in alliterative blank verse. Commonly it is reckoned a fourteenth-century

product. But the only text occurs in the Percy Folio, about
1650, and the language is not fourteenth-century. Only
two things warrant dating it before the fifteenth century,
so far as I can see: the convention that good alliterative
poems must belong to the high tide of the renaissance in
alliterative verse, and the subconscious practice of despoil-
ing the fifteenth century to enrich its predecessor. To ex-
emplify the latter practice, let me instance the best of the
anthologies, Kenneth Sisam's admirable *Fourteenth-Century Verse and Prose*. The book has seventeen selections,
chosen primarily for their high quality. But of these, three
may be questioned on date. The Towneley play occurs in a
manuscript of 1475, and it is usually reckoned that this
play was written about 1425. The translation of Mandeville
is agreed to have been written a little before 1420; there is
a second translation which was done somewhat later, but
there is no fourteenth-century English translation at all.
The Destruction of Troy, a splendid and vast alliterative
poem, survives in a single manuscript, late fifteenth-century in date. Dating the lost original in the fourteenth
century has never seriously been justified.

The fifteenth century, in fact, was richer and more
varied in its literary output than the histories usually
show. One area of its neglected contribution I shall reserve,
for the moment; it is enough to say now that it is large and
important. It would be foolish to pretend that the century
produced many brilliant writers; but it is fair to maintain
that it has suffered from scholarly behavior that is
prompted by the cyclic view of history. Its originalities
are mostly ignored—even Occleve and Lydgate have many
small novelties—and little attention is paid to its increased
cosmopolitanism. Partly because of our disposition to
reckon the date of composition as more significant than
the continuing life of a literary work, we are led into partial judgments about the taste of the period. On the basis

of its rhetorical praises, we declare that it liked Chaucer for wrong reasons; we ignore the wider expressions of its judgment which are shown in its borrowings and even more in its copying. Were it not for the sound taste of the fifteenth century, in fact, we might have no copies at all of Chaucer, or Langland, or the *Morte Arthure,* or many another fourteenth-century masterpiece. And when we do find things to praise in its writers, somehow we manage to transfer the credit elsewhere. In the copying and in the dramatic and poetical enlivening of Corpus Christi cycles, in the writing of the more truly dramatic morality plays, the fifteenth-century contribution is vital. But our historical practice is to submerge this originality in the lengthy story of an expanding *quem quaeritis* which began centuries before.

A favorite way of cutting down the period, however, is the device of anticipations. Thus, Fortescue is said to anticipate Tudor political thinking; Hawes's more musical lines foreshadow Spenser; Tiptoft, having been to Italy, is a remarkably premature swallow of the Renaissance. Or we will make an author a man for no season. Malory's achievement, according to Eugène Vinaver, lies in his having inspirations and a style that did not belong to his time. Sometimes the device even has an author going two ways. Lydgate, for example, is made to live in a revolving door; either his works head back beyond Chaucer or they show humanistic modernity not to be expected in so fifteenth-century a worthy.

The literary fifteenth century will never seem brilliant. But if we were to take a leaf from synchronic linguistics, if we were to credit the century with all that it did in an *état de littérature,* our feeling for it might change considerably from the mourner's mood that I believe is a predisposition of cyclic thinking.

But let me quit historical patterns and turn to something

quite different. Students of medieval literature, it is always pleasing to reflect, are never narrow specialists; within their capacities, and, may I say for myself, sometimes beyond them, they are eager to take a large part of all literary mankind to their bosoms. Necessity, but also conviction and delight, impel them beyond literary nationalism. Histories of medieval literature habitually tend to recognize wider relationships than do histories of later literature; it is unthinkable to write even briefly of *Sir Gawain and the Green Knight* without tracing its connections with Irish and French literature and with the Latin literature of piety and legend. But within this admirable universality, there is also a most contradictory narrowness. To illustrate the paradox, may I restrict myself to my own bailiwick?

The European fame that England enjoyed in the eighth century, and enjoyed deservedly, is represented more by its Latin writers than by *Beowulf*, splendid as that poem is. But that is not the emphasis of the English literary histories. Bede is not to be denied, nor Alcuin, and room may be found to mention the Latin verses of Aldhelm and Boniface. In its amplitude, the *Cambridge History* can spare a whole chapter for Latin writings. But normally the emphasis and the interest are almost entirely directed toward things written in English. Aelfric's Latin writings are subordinated to his English translations; where no space can be spared for the eloquent Latin lives of Boniface and Willibald, space can be found for the rough-cast Blickling *Homilies*. And in the twelfth century, if a student were anxious to know what part Englishmen played in Haskins' Renaissance, he would find plenty in Raby's Latin histories (though far from all, and little about prose), but almost nothing in a history of English literature. Geoffrey of Monmouth, too, is inescapable; he is essential to the genres that lead to Wace, Layamon, the *Morte Arthure*, and *Sir Gawain*. But what of John of Salisbury, Neckham,

Vinsauf, Nigel Longchamps, Serlo, Hillary, and the rest? What also of the many men who wrote in French? What, indeed, of those French writers, Wace, Marie, even Chrétien, whose work owes something to a cross-Channel stimulus? In a large-scale history, Anglo-Latin and Anglo-French writers may be acknowledged, but separately, in a corner, not as Englishmen writing Latin or French side by side with Englishmen who wrote English. And in a smaller history they may be ignored altogether. The result is that although the total literary scene for the English twelfth century is not incommensurate with the political scene— it is probably the most expansive period in medieval English history—the literary histories, restricting themselves to works written in English and tying even those works to pre-Conquest tradition, make it seem strangely impoverished. And what is true of these periods is also true of others, not only in England, but in other lands too.

In short, for all their internationalism, medievalists instinctively write literary history in the spirit of linguistic nationalism. When Englishmen first began to identify their national nature and pride with their national vernacular is not certain; I suspect this identification has a very long history indeed, for I think I can recognize its echo in Bede. But it came to the surface during the fifteenth century, and in the sixteenth it became a battle cry.

Let me shift to matters more delicate. Among the many burdens of a literary historian is the fact that he is charged with aesthetic discrimination as well as with history. Indeed, if he gets unduly historical, it is likely that his work will be devoured by some zealously aesthetic Bicorne or Chichevache. Military and political historians, I have noticed, write more about Aelfred the Great than they do about Aethelred the Unready. But I don't think that they are dissuaded into near silence by the fact that their kings or statesmen or generals happen to be mediocre or incom-

petent. That, however, is not so in literature. There, the
best is enemy to the good, and it is deadly to the less than
good. I do not know where my reader would place John
Gower in a hierarchy of aesthetic evaluations; but consider
James Russell Lowell's comment when he compared him
with Chaucer: Gower "is the undertaker of the fair medi-
æval legend, and his style has the hateful gloss, the seemingly unnatural length, of a coffin." The ordinary historian
is rarely so witty or so crass as that; but he still proportions
his space and frames his commentary according to present-
day aesthetic judgments. And in so doing, he quite often
has to ignore the medieval popularity or importance of the
works that he is discussing. *Cursor Mundi, Prick of Conscience,* the *Ovide moralisée,* for example, survive in so
many extensive, and expensive, manuscripts, that it is evident that in their own day they must have been prized and
important literary works. But the best a literary historian
can do by them is simply to state this fact, and sometimes he
does not even do that. Chaucer and Dante are written about
endlessly; at times, one wonders whether even these giants
can support a single critic more. But a critical article on a
minor writer is something rare; and were it not that the
Early English Text Society was once motivated by an interest that pays small heed to cycles or aesthetics—an interest
in the language, that is—we might not even have editions of
some historically important medieval writings. In the
bibliographies, certainly, they are represented by very
little beyond those editions.

No one should quarrel on aesthetic grounds with this emphasis; as ordinary readers, we are always going to value or
neglect older literature as it happens to appeal or not to
appeal to our own tastes. But history is not the same thing
as aesthetics, even though aesthetics is a proper subject for
history. A political historian doesn't have to like the past
to be interested in it, and to him, a failure can well be as

interesting as a success. The literary historian, however, because of his traditional double duty, is predisposed to be the historian of successes that we still approve. The result is that he is not only uncommunicative about former successes that we now count as failures; he is also most reluctant to talk much about that important and fascinating subject, the qualities and characteristics of literary mediocrity and badness.

Underlying his procedure is a belief in universals: a belief that what we admire in Chaucer or Walther or Juan Ruiz was always admirable, that what makes the *Prick of Conscience* or the *Pèlerinage de la vie humaine* boring was tedious even in its own medieval day. The proposition may be accepted in particular instances, and still be unacceptable as a generality. The evidence is undeniable that the prose *Tristan* and the prose *Lancelot* were in no wise so deadly to medieval readers as they now are even to specialists in medieval romance. But why they were once so popular is something at which we can now scarcely guess. Many once-pleasing things there must be in their themes, ideas, style, presentation which now escape us. We have very few analyses of medieval aesthetics, of the medieval criteria relating to literary content and form which would help us to understand why this work or that was aesthetically a failure, a mediocrity, or a success in its own day.

Nor, indeed, do we have a lot of other things proper to historical study of medieval literature: studies of the conditions in which medieval writers were trained and worked or of the audiences and patrons whom they tried to please, for example. Such information is not easy to obtain, though a few recent essays have shown that it is not impossible. Ingenuity and hard work could enlighten us in many areas. And since no one has ever doubted the ingenuity or the diligence of historians of medieval literature, the neglect may perhaps be laid at the door of a convention—the convention that a literary historian must double as an *arbiter elegantiarum* for modern tastes. And while this remains so, we shall not only continue to be unsatisfied as historians; we shall also remain uncertain in any suspicions we may harbor that some of the subtle reasons that are now advanced for the success of, say, Chaucer or Malory or *La Mort Artu* may not have been reasons that would have occurred to their immediate audiences or even to the writers themselves.

Finally, one difficulty in the study of literature is the uncertainty where to draw the limits of the subject. If there is any principle at all—and the unbelievably varied offerings in the universities makes one doubt that there is—it is something that is represented by the embarrassingly old-fashioned phrase *belles lettres*. But which *lettres* are *belles,* which not *belles* enough, is always a nagging problem, and a variously settled one. About poetry and prose fiction we seldom have doubts; but thereafter we enter a penumbra of gathering darkness, from essays and biographies to histories, diaries, letters, autobiographies, sermons, travel books, works on philosophy, politics, science, economics. The histories contain representatives of all these, but how some of them get in and why, and what led to the exclusion of the rest, provides a fascinating insight into the changing complex of tradition, judgment, and whim.

This uncertainty, applied to medieval literature, has had the strangest results. Let me list just a few. Most of Christine de Pisan's poetry has been published in good scholarly editions; most of her enormous prose output is accessible only in manuscript. If a student wishes to read the most popular of all medieval romances, the prose *Tristan*, he will have to read it in one of the many medieval copies. If he be curious to check the validity of Vinaver's assertion that Malory could not possibly owe his novelties to any fourteenth-century French romancer, he will have to make almost every check from manuscripts. Medieval prose chronicles, commonplace books, letters, diaries, wills have been published extensively; but the publishers have been political or social historians, scholars who are interested in history rather than in aesthetics. Almost every scrap of medieval English poetry has been put into print, even the jingles of bookplates; but there is a tremendous amount of English prose that is mutely awaiting recognition of any kind: critical, editorial, even bibliographical. The impediments are serious: this is mostly fifteenth-century work, work of the cyclic penumbra. It is also prose, prose of the aesthetic penumbra—treatises on politics, medicine, science, law, religion, saints' lives. Under the inspiration of R. W. Chambers, serious attention is now being paid to one branch of this work. But there is also a good deal of excellent writing along other lines which merits publication, merits it even on stylistic grounds. I would cite several good translations of Alain Chartier's work, the stylistically impressive political writings of John of Ireland, and certainly the splendid version of the *Legenda aurea;* from what they know of the latter through Caxton, some people rank its narrative with Malory's. There may well be others as good. As for the many lesser works, opinions might differ as to whether they be *belles lettres.* But they are witness to the ideas and opinions and tastes that their authors thought worthy of putting on paper, and they are not totally irrelevant to *belles lettres.* For example, to write testaments, charters, and epistles in verse is a late medieval fashion. Is it totally unrelated to the new practice of writing the serious counterparts in the vernaculars?

That my generalizations might stand naked, and so provocative, I have omitted mention of various mitigating articles and studies that we all know. My task has been to set up the butts. I shall hope that not too many arrows are aimed at me. But if it is my butt that they hit, I shall comfort myself in the reflection that the utility of butts is to sharpen the aim, and the sport, of medieval marksmen.

II

DANTE'S ULYSSES AND THE MYTHIC TRADITION

Phillip W. Damon

Y TOPIC is classical myth in the *Divine Comedy;* my principal exhibit is the last voyage of Ulysses recounted in Canto XXVI of the *Inferno;* and my opening remarks consist of a brief effort to placate Nemesis. I have read Kenelm Foster's caveat to Dantologists about "the mild raillery that attends those who persist in offering solutions of problems apparently worked to death." I suppose that the last voyage does not belong to quite the same venerable class of cruxes as the identity of the DXV and the *Veltro* or the meaning of the cord that failed to snare the leopard. It is not, however, as far removed from them as one might wish. Ulysses' fatal journey into southern waters, with its swift, wholly unhomeric conclusion near the mountain of Purgatory, has been interpreted in breadth and in detail by a large number of scholars representing a great multiplicity of viewpoints. So I think that I had best begin by stating as baldly as possible what I conceive that one more interpretation might possibly add to the general understanding of Dante's relation to the mythic tradition which did so much to shape his art and his intellectual life. Dante, we ordinarily say, *used* classical myth in the *Commedia*—a phrase that perhaps implies a shade too heavily the image of a poet evoking hallowed associations from a distant literary tradition in the manner of a Boileau or a Collins. I think that there is something to be gained from entertaining the rival or at least the supplementary image of a poet who considered himself to be, and in a way *was,* not simply a user of classical myth but a maker of classical myth. Or, to put the matter somewhat less paradoxically, a poet who was continuing, rather than simply drawing on, the imaginative and intellectual processes that had been the essence of the mythic tradition in Antiquity. A mythic theme or motif is often a good deal more capacious and various and tenacious than the sum of its literary embodiments. "I miti vivi di varianti," writes Angelo Brelich—"Variants are the life of myth." A mythic theme is alive as long as it keeps changing, as long as it retains its flexible, polymorphic character, altering its personae, its locale, its incidents, its cultural implications. When some canonical literary form of the myth imposes itself and inhibits this sort of change, literature may be the gainer, but the myth, as myth, has lost one of the sources of its strength. A live myth, one that is still changing its shape and its meanings, has a kind of continuity that transcends the literary and cultural discontinuities that we usually have in mind when we contrast the Middle Ages with classical Antiquity. Dante's classical myths were still alive; at least they seemed alive to him. And this is one of the most important facts about them.

When Lenormant was excavating at Eleusis in the 1860's, he was intrigued by the veneration of a local saint, Hagia Dhimitra, who was conspicuously absent from the Church's calendar. He asked about her history, and a priest (who claimed to be 114 years old) told him the story of how Dhimitra once had a very beautiful daughter and how a cruel Turkish aga from the neighborhood of Souli had fallen in love with her and carried her off one Christmas while Dhimitra was at church. Dhimitra hunted everywhere for her daughter and finally found her with the

assistance of a herdsman from Eleusis. In gratitude to the
city that had helped her, she invoked a blessing on its fields,
and they have been fertile ever since. It would be misdiag-
nosing the situation a little to say that the Eleusinians were
using classical myth. They were telling a story that had a
vitally important etiological connection with the central
concerns of the community. The story was an old one,
even as it had been when Hesiod told it. The myth of
Demeter and the Kore had, in other words, been doing for
the first eighteen centuries of the present dispensation
exactly what it had done under the previous one. It had
maintained its vitality by changing its content while re-
taining its fundamental theme. Its transmission had very
probably been unbroken. The connection between the
modern and ancient versions was an organic one, the result
of a continuous process of adaptation, accretion, and as-
similation. Dante's relation to his ancient mythological
sources was not entirely unlike this.

I have a distinct impression that efforts to understand
the tradition behind figures like Dante's Ulysses usually
focus somewhat too narrowly on the literary canon and on
explicit ancient and medieval comment about the canon.
Everyone knows, to be sure, that Dante's conception of
such figures was a composite one which had filtered down
through many centuries of reinterpretation, misunder-
standing, Christianization, moralization, and so forth; but
critical analysis has not always been very thoroughly informed by this knowledge. It would be possible to cite
studies that have done adequate justice to the density and
the vagueness of Dante's mythological learning and to the
complexity of its transmission. But the tendency has been
to discuss the background of passages like Ulysses' last
voyage by gathering literary citations, narrative analogues,
and parallels without attending much to the mythic theme
and its meanings or to the conceptual constants that under-

lay these specific literary sources and found expression in
many forms without losing their integrity or continuity
as a leading idea.

You will recall that Dante and Vergil had reached the
first *bolgia* of the eighth circle, the abode of the Evil Coun-
selors, and had, with some trepidation on Dante's part,
approached the double flame which enwrapped the spirits
of Ulysses and Diomedes. "Move not away," says Vergil to
the flame:

> "Let one of you relate
> How, being lost, he went away to die."
>   The greater portion of that ancient flame
> Began to writhe and murmur as it writhed,
> As will a fire when beaten by the wind.
> Then, waving its extremity about,
> As though it were the flame's own tongue that spoke,
> From out its depth it sent a voice that said:
> "When I escaped from Circe, near Gaeta,
> Where she had kept me hidden for a year—
> Before Aeneas had so named the place—
> Neither the tenderness I bore my son,
> Nor filial piety, nor yet that love
> Which should have gladdened my Penelope,
> Sufficed to overcome my eager wish
> To gain experience of the world, and learn
> The vices and the virtues of mankind.
> So I put forth upon the open sea
> With but a single ship and that small band
> By whom I never yet had been deserted.
> I saw the coasts on either hand, as far
> As Spain, Morocco, and Sardinia,
> And other islands, lying in that sea.
> I and my men were old and broken down
> When we arrived before that narrow strait
> Where Hercules of old set up his marks,
> As signs that man should never venture farther.
> Upon the right I left Seville behind,
> And on my other hand passed by Ceuta.
> 'Brothers,' I said, 'who now have reached the west

By conquering a hundred thousand dangers,
Deny not to that little span of life—
The brief allotment of your waking hours
That yet remain to you—experience
Of that unpeopled world beyond the sunset.
Consider from what noble seed you spring:
You were created not to live like beasts,
But for pursuit of virtue and of knowledge!'
  "So eager to set out I made my men
By this short speech, that after it was spoken
I would have tried in vain to hold them back.
When we had turned our poop toward the dawn,
Winged by our oars for our insensate flight,
We worked our vessel more and more to port.
At night I now could see the strange new stars
That guard the other pole—and ours so low
It did not rise above the ocean floor.
Five times the light beneath the moon was kindled
And then put out as many times again,
While we coursed o'er the highways of the deep,
When there appeared to us a murky cliff.
It loomed afar and seemed exceeding high—
Higher than any I had seen before.
Our sudden joy to weeping soon was turned;
For from this land, a whirlwind now uprose
And smote upon the forepart of our ship.
Three times it whirled us round with all the waters:
The fourth, it made the poop rise in the air,
The prow go down—as was Another's will—
Until the ocean had closed over us."

Look in almost any modern commentary, and you will be told that Dante invented this story. From a number of possibilities, I read four representative comments in ascending order of assertiveness: (1) "does not agree with the *Odyssey,* and is thought to be Dante's invention"; (2) "derives from no classical source, and appears to be Dante's invention"; (3) "entirely Dante's invention"; (4) "purely Dante's invention." Opinion on this point has not changed substantially since Benvenuto da Imola, observing

that every schoolboy knew about Ulysses' death on Ithaca
at the hands of Telegonus, wrote that Dante's account was
a calculated and wholly original feat of poetic imagination:
"Hoc auctor de industria finxit, et licuit fingere de novo."
This is not to say that there has been a lack of research into
the sources of individual details in the passage. Among the
authorities on whom Dante is alleged to have drawn are
Seneca, Horace, Statius, Pliny, Quintus Curtius, Servius,
Claudian, Augustine, Dares and Dictys, Guido delle Co-
lonne, and Solinus. In addition, there is no doubt that
Nardi was right in suggesting that Cicero's praise in the
De Finibus of Ulysses' "inborn love of knowledge" must
have informed Dante's picture of the hero setting out on
his final quest for virtue and knowledge. But none of these
sources takes us very far; they remain a set of disjointed
details whose relevance to Dante's narrative is minor and
tenuous. An accurate estimate of their bearing on the passage is given by Paul Renucci in his book *Dante, disciple et
juge du monde gréco-latin*. Renucci also calls the passage
an invention—a term that you may have gathered I am
not fully prepared to accept—but he is right about the
relative unimportance of the sources usually cited. "Such,"
he writes of the voyage,

> is the extraordinary legend invented by Dante. Invented,
> we say, because even though one can find here and there in
> classical literature lines and phrases which might have fur-
> nished a point of departure for the poet's imagination, the
> adventure itself has no precedent. Posthomeric legend pro-
> vided Ulysses with a number of supplementary exploits and
> miscalculations, but no one before Dante imagined this
> grand and tragic voyage toward a secret world forbidden
> to the living, where the mountain of Purgatory rises.[1]

Now, this observation about the story's lack of precedent is correct in the narrow sense that Dante was clearly

[1] Paul Renucci, *Dante, disciple et juge du monde gréco-latin* (Paris,
1954), p. 210.

the first to construct this narrative version of Ulysses' death. If what is meant by "precedent" is an ancient or medieval statement that a hero named Ulysses deserted a lady named Penelope to sail to the land beyond the sunset, ultimately reached the Southern Hemisphere, and sank near the foot of a mountain called Purgatory, then there is no such precedent. But if the definition of precedent is expanded to mean an intellectually viable, formally related group of motifs and ideas that were associated in Dante's mind with the name of Ulysses, then there is ample and fairly precise precedent for the major part of his narrative. The fact that no commentator will tell us about it is what comes of thinking too narrowly in terms of names and specific narrative incidents, and equating these with the mythic tradition. Dante's view of the tradition was a good deal broader and more vital than this. He was, to use a phrase of Ezra Pound's, "gathering a live tradition from the air," and its life lay not just in the scraps of information he could discover in the authors he knew, but in the theme that gave coherence to his information.

In discussing this theme, I shall have to begin at the beginning, that is, with the *Odyssey*, even though Dante had no direct, and very little accurate indirect, knowledge of that poem. It is no longer entirely respectable to talk very seriously about solar myth in the *Odyssey*. Several scholarly generations wasted so much time arguing whether periegetic heroes like Odysseus and Jason and Hercules were or were not faded sun gods that the genetic question (which has the double disadvantage of being unanswerable and not very interesting) came to be thought of as *the* question; and when no good answers were forthcoming, the whole matter tended to be irritably dismissed. And yet, since there are important solar motifs in the *Odyssey* and since they bear on my argument, I shall have to swallow my pride and mention them. The journey of the sun toward

the sunset region, the Kingdom of Osiris, lord of the West-
erners, was a dominant narrative theme of Egyptian myth,
and elements from it were borrowed, early and late, by
Greek poets. The Argonauts began their homeward journey
from the land of Aietes, son of Helios—the region where,
according to a tradition as old as Mimnermus, the king's
chamber was full of golden sunbeams. From this island far
to the east, they sailed westward and finally passed the
Gates of Night to reach, far to the west, the island of Helios' daughter Circe whose husband, according to the tradition Vergil knew, was Picus, the Woodpecker, ruler of
what Callimachus called the *arche dyseos,* the Kingdom of
the Sunset. Ulysses, whose journey home has so many
points of contact with the Argonautic expedition, touched
at several sunrise and sunset lands, among them Circe's
isle, which in his version lies toward the east, where the
dawn has "her dwelling and her dancing grounds." The lore
of Ithaca, the western terminus of Ulysses' wanderings,
contains many subtle indications that it has been mytho-
logically assimilated to the region of the sunset. In Egyptian myth, the sun-god passed through the western Gate of
the Sun asleep in the solar boat that carried him across the
world in the course of a day. The Phaeacian boat that
brings Ulysses to Ithaca can magically steer itself any-
where in the world in a single day, and as he steps into
it he immediately falls into a deep sleep. (Once before, as
he had caught sight of Ithaca after leaving Aeolus' island,
he had, rather strangely, fallen asleep.) "Ithaca," says
Ulysses to the Phaeacians, "lies well out toward the *zophos*
—the sunset—while the neighboring islands of Doulichium, Same, and wooded Zacynthus lie nearer the rising
sun." This description is notoriously incompatible with the
geography of the Enchiniades islands, which are strung
along an axis bearing approximately 350 degrees. Argu-
ments designed to prove that Homer was thinking of

Leukas, or of Theaki, or of Corfu have been subtle, passionate, and protracted, but none of them really works. I think
it likely that Homer (whatever he may or may not have
known about the geography of the western Archipelago)
put Ithaca toward the sunset for the same reason he may
have taken Doulichium, which lies "nearer the rising sun,"
away from Meges, who rules it in the Iliad, and installed as
head of its first family a man who bears the name of one of
the more notable sun-kings of Greek myth—Nisus, the
Shining One. He was probably thinking of mythological
rather than geographical configurations at the moment.
Aristotle, in a fragment of his lost *Constitution of the
Ithacans,* provides a glimpse of the popular tradition by
reporting that Eumaeus succeeded his master as ruler on
the island, and that he and his men founded a clan called
the Koliadae, the sons of Kolios. The word *kolios* occurs in
Aristotle as a variant of *keleos,* which means woodpecker;
and nothing is more likely than that the westernmost of
the Western Isles should have been ruled, in some local
legend or other, by an embodiment of the King Keleos of
mainland myth, who was so closely connected with the
Picus who lived in the Kingdom of the Setting Sun and on
the island of the Sun's daughter, far to the west. Many of
the posthomeric westward journeys of Ulysses were toward
regions with the same mythological associations as Ithaca's.
The *Telegony* was virtually a pastiche of solar motifs.
Ulysses was always, in the mythological sense, bound toward some western region that was the home of sleep,
death, and the setting sun.

The subsequent developments of this mythological theme
did not occur in the narrative tradition. Dante did not need
to have access to Homer or the *Telegony* or the Byzantine
commentators in order to know that Ulysses was a voyager
toward the western end of the sun's course, the Gates of
the Sun. Porphyry, Numenius, and other Neoplatonic phi-

losophers constructed large-scale cosmological allegories in
which the Gates of the Sun were specifically associated with
the goal of Ulysses' homeric wanderings, and were, in fact,
located on Ithaca. Their speculations on this point were
faithfully reproduced by Macrobius in his commentary on
the *Somnium Scipionis*. The major datum in this allegorical
tradition was the Cave of the Nymphs near which Ulysses
awakens on Ithaca and in which he hides his treasure and
later confers with Athena. Among its several peculiarities,
the cave had two entrances, one for men and one for gods.

> Its entrances are two, one
> On the side where the North Wind strikes, through
>   which mortals descend,
> The other on the side where the South Wind blows,
>   a sacred
> Way through which none pass but immortal feet.

One of the more puzzling features in the syncretic cos-
mologies of late Antiquity was the transfer of the sunset
region, the land of darkness and the starting point of the
sun's night journey, away from the west to the south. This
relocation of the Gates of the Sun did not have any great
impact on medieval cosmology, but it had a considerable
vogue for a while. It probably represented a temporary effort to harmonize the Greek and Egyptian location of
Hades in the west with the Babylonian scheme, which
located it in the south. But whatever the reason, Homer's
Cave of the Nymphs became a locus for the theory that
the Gate of Night, which the epic tradition had put in the
west, was really located in the Southern Hemisphere,
under the Tropic of Capricorn, where the sun goes down
in the sense of reaching its lowest point on the ecliptic.
When Hermes, in the last book of the *Odyssey*, led the
suitors past the Gates of the Sun to the Land of the Dead,
he led them, of course, out over the ocean to the west. It
was this region, or rather the mythological ideas associated

with it, which Neoplatonic allegory connected with the southern entrance to the Cave of the Nymphs, which was held to symbolize the Tropic of Capricorn. "Capricorn and Cancer," wrote Macrobius in his account of the Cave of the Nymphs, "are called the Gates of the Sun because at each of these points the sun reaches the extreme limits of the course from which it never departs." Ithaca's traditional connection with the sunset may have encouraged this allegorical identification of the cave with the Gates of the Sun, and thus produced the idea that Ulysses, while sailing westward toward the sunset, was, in a higher sense, bound for the Southern Hemisphere.

So Dante's Ulysses sets out to reach the land beyond the sunset, heads his ship due west, and then (without explanation) begins to work his ship gradually to port until he reaches the Southern Hemisphere. The likelihood that Dante was following the complexities of the Neoplatonic tradition seems to me to rise to a fair certainty when we consider that the same authors who identified the Tropic of Capricorn with the southern entrance to the cave, also associated it with the great pagan counterpart of purgatory, the region of the descent, purification, and ascent of souls, described by Plato in the tenth book of the *Republic*. According to Porphyry in his treatise, *De Antro Nympharum*, it was under the Tropic of Capricorn, at the southern gate of the sun (which is to say, allegorically, at the southern entrance to the cave) that souls, purged of the dross of earthly existence, become light again and rise toward the starry heaven. Macrobius wrote:

> Through these gates of the sun, souls are believed to enter earth from the heavens and to return from earth to heaven. Consequently, one of them [Homer's northern entrance] is called the gate of men, and the other [Homer's southern entrance] the gate of the gods. Cancer is the gate of men because this is where the descent occurs. Capricorn, how-

ever, is called the gate of the gods because through it souls return to the seat of their immortality and join the number of the gods. And this is what Homer, with divine insight, signified in his description of Ulysses' cave on Ithaca.

So the broad image of a journey toward the sunset, which became a journey toward a point in the Southern Hemisphere at which purged souls rise to heaven, was given to Dante. It was not given as a series of concatenated incidents, but as an idea which Dante, like a good maker of myth, expressed in terms of narrative.

An awareness of the mythic tradition behind Ulysses' last voyage provides, I believe, a firmer hold on the meaning of his destruction, and that of his crew, "as pleased Another"—"Another" being, of course, the God whose name none of the damned can utter. There has been much scholarly argument about the theological implications of the shipwreck. Was it divine punishment for an act of intellectual presumption? Was Ulysses' exhortation to follow knowledge and virtue even beyond the Pillars of Hercules an instance of the evil counsel that sent him to the eighth circle? A number of scholars have thought so, and the fascicles of the *Lettura Dantis* series devoted to Canto XXVI practically constitute a running debate on this question. Renucci, in the book I have already mentioned, and Yvonne Batard, in her *Dante, Minerve, et Apollon*, emphatically side with what I suppose is now the majority opinion: that Ulysses is damned, as Dante says he is, for his role in the taking of Troy, and that his voyage has nothing to do either with punishment or with his damnation. "The shipwreck is not a punishment," writes Miss Batard. "Ulysses is punished as a liar, not as a seeker after truth. . . . Ulysses had no intention of committing a sacrilege; he was not rebelling against a law he did not know. The shipwreck means simply that man cannot, by using human resources, pass from the natural to the supernatural world."[2] Renucci asks, "What connection is there between this last voyage and the Trojan Horse, the theft of the Palladium, and the discovery of Achilles on Scyros? The passage is a digression . . . the symbol of a humanity without God which mistakenly attributes its own weakness to timidity rather than to blindness."[3] Against such views, it has always been argued that no other inhabitant of Dante's otherworld tells a long story that is entirely unconnected with the reasons for his eternal fate, and that there is a certain a priori unlikelihood that Ulysses should be the single exception. He does, after all, cajole his men into passing beyond the pillars set up to discourage such enterprises, and this was evidently bad advice or even, if one wishes to place the worst construction on the matter, evil counsel. I think that my suggestions about the solar background of Ulysses' sunset journey may offer a new, and perhaps clearer, view of this problem.

First of all, Dante seems to have associated Ulysses' voyage, at least in a general way, with the Fall of Man. In Cantos XXVI and XXVII of the *Paradiso,* we find the following sequence of events: Dante encounters the soul of Adam and is provided with answers to his unspoken questions about the primal sin, most notably the question of what the sin really consisted in.

> "My son, 'twas not the tasting of the fruit
> Which was the cause of that great banishment,
> But only the transgression of the bound."

This statement that the Fall was due to man's inability to keep to the limits set for him is followed by St. Peter's powerful reflections on what was for Dante the most signal contemporary symptom of mankind's postlapsarian failure to recognize the paths sacramentally marked out by God: that is, the unwillingness of the Church to concern

[2] Yvonne Batard, *Dante, Minerve, et Apollon* (Paris, 1952), p. 188.
[3] Renucci, *op. cit.,* p. 211.

itself exclusively with spiritual matters and leave temporal
and political ones to temporal and political authority.

> " 'Twas not our purpose that the Christian people
> By our successor be divided thus,
> Some on the right hand, some upon the left;
> Nor that the keys entrusted to my hands
> Should e'er become an emblem on a standard
> Borne to make war on those who are baptized."

After this account of the origins and the ultimate historical
consequences of man's fatal incapacity to observe limits,
Dante looks down to earth and sees the South Atlantic
stretching before him,

> So that past Cadiz I could now discern
> Ulysses' foolish course.

We are reminded here, as elsewhere in the *Commedia,* of
the analogy that Dante saw between Adam's transgression of the bound and Ulysses' "foolish course" when he
passed

> that narrow strait
> Where Hercules of old set up his marks,
> As signs that man should never venture farther.

This analogy seems to me to be quite forcibly implied in
the account of the last voyage, but these implications have
been generally missed through lack of attention to the
traditional associations on which Dante was relying. Our
sight of Ulysses is framed by two images that contrast
with each other in a manner that is very characteristic of
Dante. He likes to surround a scene with images that recall
one another and whose differences serve as an index to what
Dante the pilgrim has learned or, on occasion, failed to
learn from his experience of the scene. As Vergil and Dante
approach the flame of Ulysses and Diomedes flickering
among the other flames of the eighth circle, the poet com-
pares the upward surge of the fire to Elijah rapt up to the
skies in his fiery chariot by the whirlwind:

As he who wrought his vengeance by the bears
Beheld Elijah's chariot at their parting,
The horses rising straight up into heaven
Too swiftly for his eyes to follow them,
So that he could see nothing but the flame
As a light cloud go soaring through the skies . . .

At one end of Ulysses' narrative, we see a flame, a light
cloud, and a whirlwind bearing Elijah upward. At the
other end we see darkness, a murky cliff, and a whirlwind
bearing Ulysses down beneath the waters. The contrast
seems purposeful enough, and, given the general context
of Ulysses' journey toward the sunset, it seems very likely
to be related to the medieval tradition that associated
Elijah's translation with the rising sun and through it with
the Resurrection, man redeemed, the new Adam. Early
Christian representations of Elijah's ascent simply took
over the iconography of Helios in his chariot. Chrysostom
complained, in fact, that the pagan poets and painters had
stolen their conception of Helios from the Old Testament
account of Elijah. Sedulius, in his *Carmen Paschale,* observed that the name of Elijah, or Elias, required only the
alteration of the accent and one letter to become Helios.
Throughout the Middle Ages and down to modern times,
Elijah remained "the prophet of the Sun," his shrines located on mountaintops like those of Helios and his cults
connected with the control of the rain and sunshine.

This contrast between the images of Elijah rising in light
and Ulysses sinking in darkness enforces the same kind of
ironic *chute* that we often find in the interviews of the
Inferno, where initial impressions of strength are inverted
at the end and shown as weakness, as the pilgrim comes to
a deeper understanding of his own sinful nature. Elijah's
association with the rising sun, as a virtually standard allegorical type of man redeemed, implies Ulysses' association
with the setting sun, as a type of fallen man. The contrast
corresponds, both in its iconography and its meanings, to

a dominant metaphor for the great historical drama that Dante located at the top of his mountain of Purgatory. The image of sunset and sunrise as a symbol of the fall and the redemption of man is so widespread in medieval literature that citing specific sources is a bit artificial. "Adam ran toward the west," wrote Severianus, "and set like the sun. Then came Christ and let him rise again from his setting. . . . In Adam was man's sunset; in Christ was his sunrise." The great Easter hymns, written on the occasion of the *dies solis*, evoke the image of the "verus sol," the "verus Apollo," who became the setting sun of fallen man and went down to darkness: "occasus Christi, passio Christi." But as Prudentius wrote in his great paschal hymn, Christ rose from the waters of Acheron as the *sol iustitiae*, and man rose with him. The conceptual link between Adam's metaphorical "race toward the west" and Ulysses' journey toward the sunset emerges clearly enough, I think, from Canto XXVI.

Seeing Ulysses not just as an instance of natural man's weakness or as an exemplar of the pagan search for wisdom, but specifically as a type of Adam, fallen man, helps to resolve the questions surrounding the meaning of his fate. Dante's view of classical myth and ancient history was, of course, perfectly adjusted to the standard exegetical theory that all pre-Christian history, Jewish and Gentile alike, was one vast prefiguration of the central truths of Christianity. On this view, it was perfectly possible and indeed normal for a piece of history, whether sacred or profane, to have a meaning completely appropriate to its own time and cultural context, and also to present, for the inspection of the Christian, a set of equally objective meanings which were not accessible to the persons who made that piece of history. It was a commonplace of medieval biblical interpretation that God caused men in the state of the Old Testament to suffer fates that were judicially adequate to the state in which they were born, and yet had allegorical meanings which could be adequate only to a person who was in possession of Christian revelation. So it is quite possible to maintain that Ulysses' exhortation to his men is not an instance of evil counsel without committing oneself to the proposition that it has nothing to do with evil counsel. Allegorically, in the consciousness of Dante the Christian pilgrim, the reasons for, and the consequences of, the last voyage were profoundly connected with the kind of knowledge Adam desired and the betrayal that resulted from that desire. I am reminded of the opening of *Sir Gawain and the Green Knight*, whose author, looking at the figure of Aeneas through the dark glass of the late medieval tradition, saw in him not only Vergil's pious slave of duty but also the man who had conspired with Antenor to betray Troy. Where we see two variant traditions, each at odds with the other, the Gawain poet saw one complex, and indeed rather mysterious, tradition that required interpretation. And so he begins his introductory survey of the mingled misery and happiness in this world, the inevitable alternation of what he calls "bliss and blunder" in human experience, by tracing it back to the time when Aeneas the noble "was tried for his treachery, the truest on earth." Many curious glosses on this passage have been offered by editors who were unaware of the medieval Aeneas; but it is clear that the poet sees an allegory on man's fallen state—the flawed nobility of Adam—in the picture of Aeneas, the noble traitor, exiled from his city and wandering until he founded the beginnings of that greater city, the second Troy, which was so closely and mysteriously connected with the coming of the second Adam. Dante's vision of Ulysses was similar. His hero was a wanderer whom some authorities praised as a sage, the perfect Stoic philosopher, the paragon of loyalty and intelligence, and whom others reviled as a base trickster, liar, and

cheat. Where we, along with W. B. Stanford in his book
The Ulysses Theme, see a complex and often contradictory
literary tradition, Dante saw one rather paradoxical figure,
and found his answers in the central paradoxes, or better,
in the central mysteries of his own Christian experience.

I think my view of this matter is supported by the
meanings that seem to cluster around another pagan wanderer who did reach Purgatory and whom Dante is at
some pains to link with Ulysses. I mean Cato of Utica,
whom Dante and Vergil meet on the shore as they climb
out of the pit. Cato speaks of the mountain as "my rocks";
Vergil refers to it as "your realm." The other souls whom
Christ had taken from Limbo during the Harrowing of
Hell were, one gathers, taken directly to glory. Cato
was installed on the mountain, which is his, I suppose, by
the same right that Robinson Crusoe's island belongs to
him. Ulysses tried and failed; Cato finally made it. Now,
Cato was not merely a pagan; he was also a notorious
suicide. His presence in Purgatory and Vergil's statement
that his salvation is assured have always been minor occasions of scandal among orthodox commentators. I am sure
that I have not exhausted the literature on the subject,
but I have nevertheless read many pages without finding a
particularly helpful comment on Vergil's reference to
Cato's suicide and the motive for it. Vergil is asking Cato
for permission to conduct Dante through Purgatory:

> "I beg you look with favor on his coming.
> He goes in search of liberty—whose worth
> One who has died for her can well appraise.
> You know, and for her sake your death was
> Sweet in Utica, where you have left the vesture
> That on the day of days will gleam so bright."

The liberty that Dante is seeking is the liberty he finally
achieves when Vergil, standing with him at the edge of
the Earthly Paradise, announces, "Your will is upright,

straight, and free." That Cato should be said to have died
for the liberty Dante is seeking can hardly be dissociated
from the heavily loaded phrase, "inennarabile sacrificium,"
which is applied in the *De Monarchia* to Cato's voluntary
death, or from the statement in the *Convivio* that no mor-
tal man is more worthy to stand as a symbol for God than
Cato. Just as Beatrice's life and death suggested to Dante's
allegorical imagination the incarnation and resurrection of
Christ, so Cato's "ineffable sacrifice" for the sake of general
liberty suggested Christ's sacrifice for the sake of mankind's
freedom. Cato presides over the region in which Dante
obtains his liberty from the bondage imposed on his will
through original sin; and the analogy between his death
and Christ's probably has as much to do with his role as do
any specific ethical considerations.

Cato directs Dante to a small reed growing on the shore
which will fit him to ascend the mountain—a fairly obvious reminiscence of Homer's moly with perhaps a trace
of Vergil's golden bough. As Vergil prepares to pick the
reed, we are reminded that this shore had once been sighted
by a traveler who did not live to tell his story:

> We went on downward to that desert shore
> Which never saw its waters sailed upon
> By any who had e'er returned from there.

And as Vergil binds Dante's forehead with the reed, we
hear again the same phrase that had accompanied Ulysses'
shipwreck—"as pleased Another." The whole first canto of
the *Purgatorio* seems to evoke the memory of Ulysses and
to suggest a conceptual nexus connecting him with Cato
and Dante and their presence on the shore off which he had
gone down. I suspect that it was no arbitrary choice that
led Dante to draw his inspiration for the central image of
Ulysses' last voyage from Lucan's account of Cato's journey to the southern reaches of Libya. In the ninth book of
the *Pharsalia,* we see Cato, the indomitable leader who has

led his faithful band to the extremities of the known
world, who exhorts them in the name of virtue to press on
through an unexplored region before they die, and who
finally leads them across trackless wastes to a place in the
Southern Hemisphere where a single temple rises from the
vast level expanse of desert. "The indomitable Cato, un-
willing to wait, dared to begin a journey through unknown
regions," writes Lucan. Cato's exhortation to his men has
exactly the ring of Ulysses' words:

> "O quibus una salus placuit mea castra secutis
> indomita cervice mori, componite mentes
> ad magnum virtutis opus summosque labores."

He led them southward for months, across regions unknown to men; the familiar constellations slipped below
the horizon; and finally, below the equator, he reached the
temple of Hammon, who, as Dante could have learned
from Macrobius, was the god of the setting sun—"quem
deum solem occidentem Libyes existimant." It is here that
Cato enunciates the proposition that runs through the
Purgatorio like a leitmotif: the limits of human knowledge
are set by God and the essence of wisdom is not to inquire
beyond them. When his men suggest that Cato ask the
oracle of the god for information about their future, or at
least request him to define the nature of true virtue, the
core of his impassioned refusal is "dixitque semel nascenti-
bus auctor quicquid scire licet." God has told man once
and for all what it is permissible for man to know. The
wise man will not inquire about matters hidden from him.
As Vergil points out to Dante:

> "Mankind, remain contented with the *quia*.
> Had everything been made manifest for you,
> No need had been for Mary to bear child;
> And you have seen such intellects divine
> Desiring fruitlessly—so that their failure
> Became their sorrow through eternity."

This is the substance of what Cato said at the southern terminus of his journey, in the region dominated by the temple of the setting sun.

Adam had transgressed the bound and metaphorically followed the setting sun. Christ had followed Adam's downward path, but had risen and furnished mankind with the great example of how to keep the bound, to conform oneself to the will of God. Ulysses had passed the limits set by Hercules, sailed toward the setting sun, and gone down seeking knowledge and virtue. Cato had undertaken an abstractly similar journey and had, before the temple of the setting sun, made his refusal to pass the limits, to inquire beyond the *quia*. Dante was very good at seeing patterns of this sort, and I suspect that behind his reminiscences of Cato in his own account of Ulysses' voyage lay the intention of contrasting two journeys that had been, in a conceptual sense, the same. These related images, patterns, and ideas involved in Ulysses' sunset journey constitute what I would be willing to call a tradition. From Homer through late Antiquity and the Middle Ages, the motif of Ulysses' voyage to the west had collected meanings that operate, either implicitly or explicitly, in the *Commedia*. The myth's various embodiments and associations cohered for Dante into a continuously developing theme which was still functioning mythically. Its variousness and its proximity to his own intellectual concerns were still capable of challenging him to handle it creatively and originally. And his originality derives some of its power from the fact that nothing is really invented, that everything has, in a way, its precedent. Dante was continuing, and not just using, a mythic theme that still had the power to change and at the same time remain the same.

III

NORMAN LITERATURE AND WACE

Urban Tigner Holmes, Jr.

*T*HESE ESSAYS are intended to have a general character, expressing methodology rather than claiming solution beyond dispute of certain specific problems. With this in mind I have chosen to direct attention toward Wace and his Norman background, hoping that a brief synthesis of the influences that surrounded him may be helpful in demonstrating my preferred method of approach.

In recent years there has been an unusual amount of activity among Old French scholars on Arthurian materials, notably the Grail; another vital subject matter has been the origins of the *chansons de geste*, particularly of the *Chanson de Roland*. Aside from the publications of the Anglo-Norman Text Society, little attention has been paid to that renaissance of Norman and Anglo-Norman literature which took place in the first two-thirds of the twelfth century. Perhaps it began even earlier: certain unique manuscripts—the Oxford *Roland*, the lost manuscript of the *Pèlerinage*, the manuscript of the early *Chanson de Willalme*—may be an indication of this renewal. On occasions when I have mentioned this idea in print, I have brought down some wrath upon my head because of a conclusion at which I only hinted; namely, that the Normans and Anglo-Normans could have had a special interest in the "continental" *chansons de geste*, even if it were only to make fun. In speaking of the romance form, one does not need to be reminded that the *matière de Rome*—*Thèbes, Eneas, Troie*—had its feet in Norman soil, and that the predecessor of the romance poets, Wace, has great importance as a representative of this time and place.

Each of us has his own methodology in the study of literature, which may not be so original as one thinks. Only last October, when I was serving on a fellowship committee, I read a recommendation by an outstanding scholar praising one of his colleagues for the originality of his approach—an approach that has been mine for years, and was first suggested to me by a symposium held at the Huntington Library in San Marino in 1939. This method is to try to be an intelligent contemporary of the author whose work we are contemplating. In following this procedure it is necessary to know well the books that the author could have read, know places where he lived and worked, picture the conditions of his everyday life, and know the problems of his society. This investigation of background can be carried quite far. I for one am concerned with the houses of the period, the money that was spent, and the people whom the author could have known.

There is a special viewpoint in such a "contemporary" approach—for which we have coined the term "parallelism." A dozen or more years ago I wrote a monograph entitled *Samuel Pepys in Paris*.[1] One can ascertain precisely the dates that Pepys was in Paris in the autumn of 1669. From various sources, information can be gathered on the state of the theater, the social life, the important events, and even the important people who were present in Paris during those weeks. Is it not reasonable to assume that Pepys participated in much of this life according to his well-known tastes? For instance, there was the great funeral of Henrietta Maria, the widow of Charles I of England. Pepys was an Englishman who took himself very

---

[1] *Samuel Pepys in Paris and Other Essays* (Chapel Hill, N.C., 1954).

seriously; he must have taken part in the proceedings. In a similar way we can postulate some of the surroundings of Chrétien de Troyes in the faraway twelfth century. It is reasonable to assume that Chrétien the clerk received some of his advanced education at Troyes (in the late 1150's or in the early 1160's according to one's preferred chronology). There were not many teachers at the cathedral school in Troyes. If Chrétien attended at all it is probable that he was acquainted with the lectures of their "big man," Peter Comestor, who was at Troyes until 1164 when he moved to Saint-Victor at Paris. Peter's works are largely unpublished today; an exception is his *Historia scolastica*.[2] Surely it would be worth the trouble to examine more closely the writings of Peter Comestor. His thought might show parallels with some of the problems in Chrétien's romances.

To put flesh upon the dry bones of fact about the early writers in Norman territory, something must be said about their concern with education for the laity—in the French language. A number of twelfth-century clerics seemed to be going out of their way to make clerical material available to those who did not read Latin effectively. We do not wish to make a warm summer out of one or two swallows, but much evidence points that way. In his life of Saint Nicholas, Wace states: "For those who have not learned their letters, and have not been intent upon learning them, for these people the clerks must demonstrate religion, telling why the Feast of each saint has been established."[3] In the same poem he says: "I wish to write a little in Romance about something which we hear in Latin, so that lay people may understand this, people who cannot understand Latin."[4] We agree with Gaston Paris that the Saint

[2] J. P. Migne, *Patrologia latina*, 198, cols. 1045 ff.

[3] Einar Ronsjö, ed., *La Vie de Saint-Nicholas par Wace* (Lund and Copenhagen, 1942), vv. 1–5.

[4] *Ibid.*, vv. 41–44.

Nicholas life is one of the poet's earliest works, if only because he is so careful to define his purpose there.[5] In a much earlier, and more elementary, text, known as the "Grant mal fist Adam," an unknown Norman author has this to say: "I have made this for the 'simple *gent*' . . . I have not done this for the lettered people, because they have enough writing and argumentation of their own. I am putting this into *romanz* for the young folk who have no letters, as they will understand better the tongue which they have spoken since childhood."[6]

Baldwin of Guines (after 1169) did not live in Normandy proper, but he was close by. His two towns of Guines and Ardres were close to Calais. He too emphasized this predilection for the reading in the vernacular of clerical material. He caused the *Song of Songs* to be rendered into French, as well as the *Life of Saint Anthony*, the larger part of a medical work, the scientific treatise of Solinus, and various other things.

> From his clerks he received divine eloquence and he communicated to them unfamiliar tales which he learned from story tellers. He is to be compared with a certain individual named Milesius in the matter of strange narration; in the adventures of noble and ignoble characters he was equal to the most outstanding minstrels. His vernacular library was in the care of Hesard of Adehen, a layman, who had read all the works therein in French.[7]

It is probable that Baldwin of Guines was the patron of a *jongleur* school. Adapters and translators, as well as those who copied out the *chansons de geste*, were obliged to have some instruction in the writing and spelling of the French language. In the psalter and grammar schools only Latin was taught. Although Wace was a magister from France

[5] Gaston Paris, review of *Rou*, ed. H. Andresen, *Romania*, IX (1880), 595.

[6] H. Suchier, ed., *Reimpredigt* (Halle, 1879), stanza 127.

[7] *Monumenta Germaniae Historica, Scriptores*, XXIV, 598, § 80.

(Paris), he must have received vernacular instruction at some stage of his study. Since he spent so much of his career in the writing of Norman verse it is possible that he, too, gave vernacular instruction on the side. The spirit of this renaissance in vernacular writing is echoed very prominently by Marie de France when she says: "I began to think of translating from Latin into *romanz;* but it would hardly be worth my time since *itant*—so many—others have set about doing it." [8] Once Norman and Anglo-Norman writers got the habit of making such adaptations, the movement carried itself by its momentum, but it is only proper to reflect upon the circumstances at the outset. Attempts to explain can only be provisional, but the first thought that comes to mind is the active spirit of curiosity and enterprise which characterized Normans and Anglo-Normans. In addition we must mention the influence of strong royal patronage and the liberal spirit of the great monasteries and cathedral chapters. In Normandy these were at Rouen, Caen, Saint-Evroult, Evreux, Bayeux, Jumièges, Fonteney, Fécamp, Bec, and Savigny. The spirited activity of the Normans has been discussed by various authorities in America, notably by Charles H. Haskins [9] and Lynn White, Jr.[10] These points I will not emphasize further at the moment, but something must be said about two of the factors I have mentioned.

I have written an article on Adeliza, the second wife of King Henry I, and on her zeal as a patron of letters.[11] Her leanings toward serious learning were very marked. Home base for her was the Benedictine abbey of Afflighem, near Alost between Brussels and Ghent. Abbot Franco of that

---

[8] Marie de France, *Prologue*, vv. 28–32.

[9] *Normans in European History* (Boston and New York, 1915); and *Norman Institutions* (Cambridge, Mass., 1925).

[10] *Latin Monasticism in Norman Sicily* (Cambridge, Mass., 1938).

[11] This article appears in A. S. Crisafulli, ed., *Linguistic and Literary Studies in Honor of Helmut A. Hatzfeld* (Wash., D.C., 1964).

abbey was an active man of letters. It was he who in 1122 escorted Adeliza to England for her wedding to the English king. She always remained faithful to Afflighem, giving it grants of land. She returned there in 1150, where she died the following year. For our purposes it would be of major importance to have a twelfth-century catalogue of this monastery, but all I have at hand is a catalogue compiled in 1643 by Dom Odo Cambier.[12] He remarks in it that only a few remains of the once-famous library have been spared: "Ecce tibi reliquias codicum manuscriptorum Bibliothecae nostrae, quasi pauculas olivas relictas in olea, in quem grassati sunt heretici, plagiarii, et nescio qui alii libriperdai." Dom Odo Cambier quotes a predecessor, Luigi Guicciardini, who had observed that the monastery possessed a "celeberrima Bibliotheca" consisting of variegated books of all kinds. The few titles cited by Dom Odo Cambier offer a variety of saints' lives and biographical titles, including lives of Bede, Columbanus, Leodegarius, and so on.

To return to Adeliza herself, shortly after her arrival in Normandy she corresponded with Hildebert of Le Mans. He addressed her as one who was "totam . . . sacris occupatam studiis." [13] This phrase might be rendered "completely concerned with serious studies" (in which we should include "popular science"). Philippe de Thaun wrote his bestiary for her, and called her a gem,[14] and Benedict, his *Voyage of Saint Brendan*.[15] She commissioned a certain David to write the life of her late husband, Henry I, which has disappeared.[16] I have made the suggestion, not

[12] *Elenchus manuscriptorum codicum Belgii,* "Indiculus librorum manuscriptorum bibliothecae monasterii Affligenensis," pp. 142–152.

[13] Migne, *Patrologia latina,* v. 171, cols. 179 ff.

[14] *Le bestiare,* ed. E. Walberg (Paris and Lund, 1900), vv. 1 ff.

[15] E. G. R. Waters, ed., *The Anglo-Norman Voyage of St. Brendan* (Oxford, 1928), vv. 1–8.

[16] Gaimar, *Estoire des Engleis,* ed. A. Bell (Oxford, 1960), vv. 6487–6488.

proved, of course, that she had a hand in encouraging the chronicler Gaimar and his patroness Dame Custance. This beautiful young queen spent much of her time at Rouen during her husband's lifetime. Rouen was the home also of the Plantagenets. With such charming and active patrons, it is not strange that there was a school of poets, good and bad, in the vicinity of Rouen. Something might be adduced to suggest that Adeliza brought from Lower Lorraine a definite taste for rhymed chronicles. This region was the home territory of Godfrey of Bouillon and his two successors in the kingdom of Jerusalem. We have reason to believe that clerks of Lorraine had special interest in chronicles of the First Crusade. Godfrey of Bouillon was celebrated in Albert of Aix's *Liber christianae expeditionis* which Molinier has described as "un monument élevé à la gloire de Godefroi de Bouillon et des croisés lorrains." [17] In his preface Albert of Aix intimates that much good vernacular history of the First Crusade was in existence before him: ". . . with timorous daring I have decided to commit to permanent form what has already been noted down by those who were present at the events." [18] His work was permanent in form because it was composed in Latin. Paul Meyer took this statement to mean that vernacular rhymed chronicles on the First Crusade existed before 1121, and so do I.

Henri Omont has remarked that an understanding of intellectual history in medieval Normandy can be gained by a study of the library holdings of the great monasteries. [19] Fortunately, we have twelfth-century book lists from Bec, Saint-Evroult, Evreux, Fécamp, Saint-Wandrille of Fonteney, and the cathedral library at Rouen. A list of later date from the cathedral at Bayeux probably includes the twelfth-century list. The catalogues of Jumièges,

[17] A. Molinier, *Sources de l'histoire de France* (Paris, 1901), II, 285.
[18] *Recueil historique des Croisades Occidentales*, IV, 265.
[19] *Catalogue général des manuscrits des bibliothèques publiques de France, Départments*, II, 379.

Savigny, and, most unfortunately, of the Abbaye aux Hommes at Caen disappeared in the seventeenth century. If the Caen catalogue had not been lost, Wace's sources would be more apparent. I will give a brief analysis of the surviving shelf lists. Works on profane subjects alone are of interest now; they were in a minority. Rouen was outstanding for its classical literature; Bec was second in this. The commonest profane writings were those of Boethius and Josephus, together with Isidor's *Etymologies*, the letters of Yvo of Chartres, and various calendars. Less popular were the Norman chronicles of Ordericus, Dudon, and others, the *Digest* of Justinian, the medieval Latin *Timaeus*, the letters of Hildebert of Le Mans, Pliny's *Natural History*, and the writings of Jordanus, Orosius, Solinus, Macrobius, and Gratian. Some notable entries have one mention only: Statius' *Thebaïs* (Bayeux), *Liber de naturis bestiarum* (Evreux), pseudo-*Turpin* (Evreux), Marbod (Saint-Evroult), Petrus Alfonsi (Bec), *Gesta Francorum* (Bec), Henry of Huntingdon (Bec), Pliny the Younger (Bec), *Vita Alexandri* and *Historia Britonum* (Bec), Suetonius (Bec), Palladius (Bec), Vegetius (Bec), *Topics* of Aristotle (Fécamp), *Histories* of Peter Comestor (Fécamp). Interesting though not profane is the *Life of Saint Nicholas* (Fécamp, Bec).[20]

Some of these Latin titles accord with what was translated by the Norman poets. For instance, Philippe de Thaun adapted his *Compoz* in either 1113 or 1121. In Sainte-Lyre at Evreux there is a *Liber Albrici de computo lune* (no. 53 in its book press) and just a few books away was a *De naturis bestiarum* (no. 59). Did Philippe de Thaun have any association with Evreux? There is also the Marbod manuscript at Saint-Evroult. Could it have been

[20] These book lists are reprinted in the *Catalogue général:* Rouen, I, x-xiv; Saint-Evroult, II, 468–469; Saint Wandrille, I, xvi-xix, Jumièges, I, xix-xxiii; Fécamp, I, xxiii-xxvii; Bec, II, 385–398; Evreux, II, 380–383.

there that the oldest Norman lapidary took form? Of course, professional poets and translators could travel from monastery to monastery, presumably on invitation. There is some information on this in the *Life of Saint Thomas Becket* by Guernes (Garnier) of Pont-Sainte-Maxence. Guernes was a Francian who wrote in England for Anglo-Norman patrons. We quote a few passages in translation. Guernes explains his method of working:

> Four years have I spent in making this; I suffered by removing sections and putting back other passages. I treated the subject first from hearsay and in this way I said many things wrongly. Then I went to Canterbury where I heard the facts. I culled the truth from the friends of Saint Thomas and from those who had served him since his childhood. . . . Some scribes stole this first romance from me before I had perfected and corrected it . . . since then many rich men have bought copies of this; those who stole it should be blamed. This new account I have corrected and completed.[21]

In an epilogue of twenty-two lines, which is accepted as genuine (although it occurs in the Paris manuscript only), we are informed how Guernes was remunerated by his patrons:

> The Abbess, sister of Saint Thomas, to her honor and that of the Saint, has given me a palfrey and clothing (not even spurs are lacking). I did not make a losing throw (at the dice) when I came to her house. Nor has she lost anything from it. She will have her recompense: everywhere, among high and low I will exalt her name. From here to Patras one cannot find a better woman. The nuns of her Abbey have all been kind to me, each one with a gift. May the Good Lord send them every day plenty of wine, bread, meat, and fish! And when their bodies are silent and abased may God have mercy on their souls. I will never again cry "Alas"—for I have served a proper lord (Saint Thomas). Because I have

[21] E. Walberg, ed., *Le vie de saint Thomas Becket* (Paris, 1936), vv. 144–152, 158–160.

often grown weary rhyming about his passion he gives me everything (all joking aside): gold, silver, clothing in my saddle bags, horses, and other valuables. . . . Odo, the good prior of Holy Trinity Abbey and his monks have rendered me much assistance. They maintained me for a year and a day, and advised me. Wherever I may go, far and wide, it will be to them that I will return.[22]

Guernes may well have been a typical professional poet of the learned kind. Not all Norman poets were of this type; many were monks resident in an abbey. But it is likely that Wace too was dependent upon his pen for much of his living. Now I will attempt to place Wace in some sort of setting.

Because of the importance of his adaptation of the *Historia regum Brittaniae,* known as the *Brut,* and because of his rhymed chronicle entitled the *Rou,* Wace has long been considered a major figure in Old French literature. Specialists in medieval literature and history have highlighted every mention of his name in even the most obscure texts. It is not easy, therefore, to make new discoveries about his life and work; but it is possible to discuss him more fully by using the method of "parallelism." In a review of Hugo Andresen's edition of the *Rou,*[23] Gaston Paris put together what are now considered the essential deductions concerning Wace's birth and career. These details have received some discussion in the past eighty years by Elizabeth A. Francis, Ivor Arnold, Einar Ronsjö of Lund, M. Malkiel-Jirmounsky, M. Dominica Legge, and my own pupil of long ago, Benjamin F. Carpenter.[24] These scholars have

---

[22] *Ibid.,* pp. 191–192.

[23] *Romania,* IX (1880), 592–614.

[24] Ronsjö, *op. cit.;* Wace, *La vie de sainte Marguerite,* ed. Elizabeth A. Francis (Paris, 1932); *Le roman de Brut de Wace,* ed. Ivor Arnold (2 vols; Paris, 1938–1940); M. Malkiel-Jirmounsky in *Revue des langues romanes,* LXIII (1928), 261–296; M. Dominica Legge, *Anglo-Norman in the Cloisters* (Edinburgh, 1950); Benjamin F. Carpenter, "The Life

weighed Gaston Paris' remarks, not agreeing entirely, but in the main they have not added much that is new to the account. The basic information on Wace comes from several passages in the *Rou*:

> I will tell you who I am: Wace from the island of Jersey. I was born in Jersey but was brought to Caen when very small, where I was put to letters. Then I was taught in France [Paris] for a long time. When I came home I spent a very long time in Caen, busying myself with the making of *romanz* [poems in the vulgar tongue]. I wrote and composed many of these. By God's help, however, and through the aid of King Henry there was given to me a prebend at Bayeux.[25]

A second passage supplements the first:

> Those who wrote about *gestes* and made histories used to receive much honor; frequently they had gifts from ladies and barons whom they honored—but at present I can spend a long time with *romanz* and *serventois* before I will find a person so generous who will allow me even the hire of a copyist for one month. They just say, "Master Wace writes well." "You ought to spend all your time writing." [26]

It is evident from these lines that Wace did not spend *all* his time as a composer in the vernacular; but he must have spent a great deal of it that way. Since he makes a contrast between *romanz* and *serventois*, it is probable that for him the term *romanz* was being shaded a little and no longer meant just anything composed in the vulgar tongue.

In the twelfth century the island of Jersey was dedicated almost entirely to agriculture. It had no castle, and no ecclesiastical setup of any general importance.[27] Wace was

and Writings of Maistre Wace" (unpublished thesis, University of North Carolina, 1930).

[25] *Rou*, ed. H. Andresen (2 vols.; Heilbronn, 1878–1879), III, vv. 5321–5338. The numeral III indicates the main poem, II, the *Chronique ascendante*, I, the introductory version by Wace.

[26] *Rou*, III, 143–159.

[27] Auguste Vacquerie, *Jersey, les miettes de l'histoire* (4th ed.; Paris, 1869).

therefore sent to some relative in Caen, where he doubtless attended psalter school and his first grammar school. His higher education was acquired in France, which meant Paris. There he obtained the grade of magister, which was a *licentia docendi*. All this can be inferred with very little guessing. Probably he studied the arts, with some canon law. From other lines, we know that he practiced as a *clerc lisant* at Caen under the three King Henrys, beginning before 1135 (when Henry I died) and continuing past 1170 (when Henry the Young King was crowned). There should be no dispute over the meaning of *clerc lisant;* it means "teacher, reader, lector." It has been difficult to cite an Old French passage defining *lisant* in the sense of "teaching," but a number can be found in the Huguet dictionary, such as: ". . . nul ne peüst lire en theologie qu'il ne fut aagé de 35 ans . . ."[28]

It is extremely doubtful that Wace was a Benedictine monk at the Abbaye aux Hommes in Caen. More likely he maintained a psalter school or perhaps a grammar school for the people of Caen who were clerically minded. He could not have "boarded" very many young students while devoting so much time to Anglo-Norman vernacular poetry. His earlier writings suggest that his chief patrons were the Abbaye aux Hommes, and the nearby Saint-Evroult (where Ordericus Vitalis was a monk until his death in 1143). Eventually Wace discovered the better possibilities to be derived from writing for the King and Queen at Rouen.

It is worthwhile to attempt a description of the surroundings in which Wace worked during his more than thirty-five years in Caen.[29] Think of twelfth-century Caen

[28] Edmond Huguet, *Dictionnaire de la langue française du 16ᵉ siècle,* s.v. *lire,* 1 (intrans.)

[29] See modern maps of Caen (before 1943); Michel Béziers, *Mémoires pour servir à l'état historique et géographique du diocèse de Bayeux* (Rouen and Paris, 1896), I, 22, 25, 26; Gabriel Vanel, *Recueil de journaux caennais, 1661–1777* (Rouen, 1904).

as a great T with a short stem and a crossbar that was un-
usually long. On top of the T there was a round hill, the
castle on which was occupied by the viscount in charge of
the town. At the left extremity of the T's crossbar was
Saint-Estienne, the Abbaye aux Hommes. This section was
the clerical district; although I have not found the term,
it was probably called Bourg l'Abbé or Bourg aux Clercs.
A large gate in the wall there led to the Bayeux road. At
the opposite extremity of the crossbar was Sainte-Trinité,
or the Abbaye aux Dames. At the junction of crossbar and
stem lay the principal secular church of Saint-Pierre. From
this junction, running south, was the Rue d'Esmeisine
(today, Rue Saint-Jean), which ended at the Porte Milet,
or Milly—a distance of some 500 yards. Just inside this
gate was the Church of Saint-Jean. Just outside, across the
road, was the Hospital of Saint-Thomas and Saint-
Antoine.[30] Once outside the gate the Esmeisine Road led
another 400 yards to the river Orne.

Wace himself lists most of these features of the town.
He mentions a big trench, dug during the last stand of
Robert Courthose in 1135. It bordered the Esmeisine Road
from the river as far as the gate.[31] Within the town, the
area near Sainte-Trinité was designated as Bourg l'Abbesse,
and the street just below it was La Rue Basse. On the opposite arm of the T, in the quarter of Saint-Estienne, there
were three good churches: Saint Nicholas (which was used
by the serving men in the abbey); Saint-Martin, close to
the north wall of the town, near Porte Arthur; and Notre
Dame de Froide Rue. (This "cold street" received its name
because there was little sunlight there). There was an open
space, a meeting ground for the citizens, between Saint-
Martin and the north wall. This area used to be an orchard
and garden. For these details we are quoting Wace.[32] There

[30] In modern times this hospital became the Hôtel-Dieu.
[31] *Rou*, III, 10,937–10,943.
[32] *Rou*, III, 11,359–11,370.

was the Oudon, a stream that ran along the principal street connecting the two great abbeys, then turned southward through the wall and served as a moat, flowing into the Orne. Situated where the Oudon and the Orne joined, the port of Caen was sixteen miles from the English Channel. It was there that so much of the Caen stone was loaded for England and elsewhere. Wace described the activity in the port at Southampton.[33] Did he have in mind also his own port at Caen? We make a controlled guess that Wace's house and school lay in the clerical district of the town, not far from the Abbaye aux Hommes or Saint-Estienne.

Close by were Saint-Nicholas and Notre Dame de Froide Rue. Wace wrote his life of Saint Nicholas for someone named Robert Tiout.[34] Was it for Notre Dame de Froide Rue that Wace wrote the poem *Conception de la Vierge?* Approval of the Feast of the Immaculate Conception, granted in England by 1129, was withheld in Normandy, where it had met considerable opposition, until 1145.[35] Wace's poem narrates how this feast came to Normandy. A kind of *puy d'amour,* or poetic competition, soon came to be associated with this feast.

At the cathedral of Bayeux there was a chapel dedicated to Saint Margaret of Antioch. When Antioch was captured in the First Crusade (1098), Saint Margaret's relics were taken to Europe and distributed among various shrines. Some explanation of her life was needed, and we may assume that Wace obliged, for a fee. He says of this saint, "Ladies should love her very much, and praise Lord God for her. May she have mercy upon our sins. Gace composed this life. He has put into *romanz* what Theodimus has written." [36] Among the thirty-two chapels at the Bayeux

---

[33] *Brut,* vv. 10,609 ff.

[34] *La Vie de Saint Nicholas,* vv. 1549–1550.

[35] Edmund Bishop, *On the Origins of the Feast of the Conception of the Blessed Virgin Mary* (London, 1901).

[36] *Vie de sainte Marguerite,* vv. 737–742.

cathedral there was one dedicated to the Immaculate Conception and another to Saint Nicholas.[37] It is not impossible that Wace wrote all three of his extant saints' lives for the cathedral chapter (in which event it would be necessary to explain the participation of Robert Tiout). I doubt that he did so and prefer to assume that these lives were composed for local use within the town of Caen.

As Wace wrote a considerable number of vernacular poems, it is curious that his lives of the saints were the only ones destined to survive—except for the *Brut* and the *Rou*. His *serventois,* or political poems, would be invaluable to us. Probably they were allowed to disappear because they were critical of the wishes of the King, and encouraged Norman opposition.

In his prologue to the main section of the *Rou,* Wace remarks, "He [the King] caused me to be given a prebend at Bayeux." [38] This prologue must have been added after 1170 since it mentions service under the three Henrys. There are important documents at Bayeux, dating from 1166, 1169, 1172, and 1174, in which Wace appears in this capacity.[39] In the 1166 and 1172 charters, the name appears as "Accius," which must be equivalent to "Waccius." If Wace was not a resident canon (and he was not, because, on his own admission, he continued to be a "clerc de Caen" after 1170), the clerk who wrote the names might well have distorted Waccius into Accius, and no one bothered to correct it. In any event, Wace was mentioned as a canon in 1169.

Most of us have not meditated on what being a canon at Bayeux might mean. In the absence of specific regulations to the contrary, Wace's prebend can be explained in this

[37] Béziers, *op. cit.,* II, 3–10.

[38] *Rou,* III, 173–174.

[39] Documents are discussed by E. du Méril in *Jahrbuch für romanische und englische Literatur,* II (1862), 214 ff., and are printed by Bourienne in *Le livre noir de Bayeux* (Rouen, 1903), I, 74, 56, 103.

way. A prebend was an endowed chair, given at the will of the king, who was the patron at Bayeux. The endowment was paid by a church, or some other foundation within the diocese. A residentiary canon was in higher orders (subdeacon, deacon, or priest) and lived in the collegiate community. On the other hand, a prebendary, or nonresident canon, could remain in lower orders and could be married; in fact, he might even be a layman and entitled to wear only the surplice and the amice. A prebendary had three regulations to follow: (1) he should reside at the church which paid his endowment; (2) he should perform the duty prescribed in his appointment; and (3) he should attend the bishop's chapter meeting, supposedly once a month. Such a prebend *ad honores* could be granted as a hereditary fief.[40] Michel Béziers records forty-nine prebends and canonicates at Bayeux. Some of these had not been established as early as the twelfth century, but in the list are three from Caen: Saint-Pierre, Notre Dame de Froide Rue, and Saint-Jean.[41] As a prebendary Wace might have continued his residence in one of these local chapters in Caen, journeying the sixteen miles to Bayeux (half a day's journey) for the chapter meetings.

The rate of work, or speed at which a twelfth-century poet could rhyme, varied considerably with the individual. From various sources I have estimated that the usual rate was from 3,000 to 5,000 lines a year. (Gaimar was a quick worker who composed the 6,000-odd lines of his *Estoire des Engleis* in thirteen months.) [42] Wace was not on the quick side. His *Brut,* with 15,300 verses, probably required four or five years for its rhyming, meaning that Wace began the poem in 1150 or 1151, when Eleanor was still the wife of Louis of France. Wace says that he completed the

[40] This material can be checked in *La enciclopedia cattolica* (Città del Vaticano, 1949–1954).

[41] See Béziers, *op. cit.*, I, 2–3.

[42] Gaimar, *Estoire des Engleis,* vv. 6438 ff.

Brut in 1155.[43] When he began this work, Geoffrey of Monmouth was still alive (he died in 1154). It is possible that Geoffrey knew of the undertaking; he may even have encouraged it. By 1155 the scene had changed: Queen Eleanor was a blithe spirit who delighted in the new styles of poetry which were in the air; and the *Brut* was something new. Layamon, at the end of the century, is our authority that Wace finally dedicated the leaves of his great poem to Queen Eleanor: ". . . the third book . . . that a French clerk made, who was named Wace, and who gave it to the noble Eleanor, high King Henry's Queen." [44] But she is mentioned nowhere in the text of the poem. We may believe that Wace began his long adaptation of Geoffrey on speculation, aware that the folk around him were ready for this kind of narrative in a popular form. Henry of Blois, abbot of Glastonbury and bishop of Winchester, was at the height of his influence at the time. The *Brut* is a subject that must have suited his tastes. It was a forerunner of the romance in form and style.

It is surprising that Wace ever undertook the *Brut*, for he was undoubtedly a sober man, a hardheaded moralist. As he observes very early in the *Rou*, not long after 1160, "Everything declines, decays, dies, comes to an end. Towers crumble, walls give way, and the rose withers. A horse stumbles, and cloth grows old; man dies, iron wears away, and wood will rot. All that is made by hand will perish." [45] What is said in the preceding quotation is certainly true, but it is hardly in the spirit of Eleanor of Aquitaine. While doing the *Brut*, Wace omitted entirely the famous prophecies of Merlin. He explained, "I do not wish to translate [this account] since I do not know how to interpret it; I would not want to say anything that is not as I myself

[43] *Brut*, vv. 14,865–14,866.
[44] *Layamon's Brut*, ed. Sir Frederick Madden, vv. 31–43.
[45] *Rou*, III, 131–136.

would tell it." [46] In the *Rou* he mentions an epic tale, but does not continue with it:

> I have heard minstrels in my childhood who have sung how William long ago blinded Osmunt and dug out the eyes of Count Riulf and how he caused Ansketil to be slain by trickery, and Balzo of Spain to be guarded with a shield. I know nothing about these, nor can I discover anything further about them. When I have no corroboration of detail I do not care to repeat nor do I wish to affirm that lies are true.[47]

Elsewhere Wace speaks of the forest of Broceliande, says that he visited the place himself and found nothing out of the ordinary there—it was just a fake.[48] So matter-of-fact an attitude makes us wonder whether Wace ever composed truly imaginative verse in those *romanz* that have been lost. But he makes some noteworthy additions to the legend of Arthur as told by Geoffrey, introducing into his *Brut* the first suggestion of the Round Table: "Arthur made the Round Table, about which the British utter many a fable." [49] He also corroborates that since Arthur's removal to Avalon, "There are still British who say and understand that he is still alive and will return from there." [50]

To put it briefly, despite his prosaic attitude toward imaginative detail, Wace helped create the romance form in his adaptation of Geoffrey of Monmouth's Latin prose. Description, conversation, development of love motifs, chivalric treatment, portrayal of character, fine use of the octosyllabic rhymed couplet—all these novelties make him cofounder of the romance type that developed after 1150 with the *Roman de Thèbes*. What manuscript of the *Historia regum Brittaniae* did Wace use? It is known that there

[46] *Brut*, vv. 7733 ff.
[47] *Rou*, I, 1361–1367.
[48] *Rou*, III, 6415–6420.
[49] *Brut*, v. 9998.
[50] *Brut*, vv. 13,685 ff.

was a manuscript with this subject matter in the library at Bec, for in 1139 Robert de Torigny showed it to Henry of Huntingdon, who summarized it sufficiently to make us believe it was one of the two versions of Geoffrey's *Historia*. Like Wace's *Brut*, Henry's résumé does not mention the prophecies of Merlin; but it includes Arthur's expected return.[51]

Wace's long unfinished poem, the *Rou*, was begun certainly in 1160,[52] at the behest of Henry II who wanted something similar to the *Brut* which would deal with his Norman ancestors. Although the *Rou* is semihistory, while the *Brut* and the first romances—*Thebes* and *Troie*—are fictitious, Wace does not claim more truth for his *Rou*. He says there has been "much new discussion" of Thebes and the "great pride" of "Troie," and so forth, but they have disappeared and only "through the clerks who have written and who have put the *gestes* into books do we know how to speak about the olden times and can retell many of the works." [53] The "repallance de Thebes" must refer to the vernacular romance—which he treats as history! Wace's main sources were Dudon de Saint Quentin, William of Jumièges, and Ordericus Vitalis. We can designate these as Ordericus and predecessors.

Four sections of the *Rou* have come down to us, and they present a puzzle. The first part has 751 octosyllabic rhymed couplets, tracing the Norman dukes as far as Rollo ("Rou"). This section may have been a first sample sent to the King. In the same sequence there follow 4,424 twelve-syllable mono-rhymed *laisses* which carry on the narrative as far as Duke Richart and King Lothair. This passage ends

[51] Robert de Torigni, *Chronicle of Stephen and Henry II*, ed. R. Howlett, Rolls Series, IV, 65 ff. See also item under "Bec library," *ibid.*, p. xvi.

[52] *Rou*, II, 1 ff.

[53] *Rou*, I, 23–40.

with the lines: "One can grow tired and one can be gay over fine songs, but he who composes must turn where he can find his hire. One must get ahead professionally. Willingly would he [Wace] acquire favor, for he needs it." [54] From this remark we may judge that Wace was tired of composing free samples for King Henry.

Another section, which consists of 315 lines in mono-rhymed twelve-syllable *laisses,* is generally referred to as the *Chronique ascendante* because it narrates in reverse order the activities of the Norman dukes from Henry II back to Rou. There is material in this part which must be dated after 1170; Gaston Paris thinks that it was interpolated. It is difficult to date this part in proper sequence, but that it was some sort of request for money is clear. After praising Henry and Eleanor the poet adds: "The King soothes me with gifts and promises, but I am often in need—need that comes very quickly and frequently obliges me to put a penny and a pledge." [55]

The main section of this poem, known as the *Rou,* has 11,502 octosyllabic rhymed couplets. At the finish, Wace breaks off abruptly and says that the King has asked Beneeit de Sainte-More to take over the project. It is generally assumed that this interruption was in 1174, meaning that Wace had taken some fourteen years to complete a grand total of 16,231 verses. Beneeit de Sainte-More did not continue Wace's work but developed from the beginning his vast *Estoire des Dus de Normandie.* He had finished 42,310 lines when he too broke off—in 1189—after the death of the King. He produced an average of 3,000 verses a year.

But we are not concerned with Beneeit except to ask: Why did Henry II prefer Beneeit for the continuation, or

[54] *Rou,* I, 4421–4423.
[55] *Rou,* II, 21–23.

rather redoing, of this huge project? It is generally believed that Wace was proceeding far too slowly—which was true. In addition, it should be noted that Wace was too favorable to Robert Courthose and the Norman cause against Henry I. The closing lines of Wace's *Rou* are rather eloquent in their opposition to Henry I.[56] We may suspect that Henry II was no longer pleased with Wace's stubbornness and *parti pris*.

If Wace had stopped principally because of age we could expect some mention of this disability. Instead he shows pique: "Some time ago the King did me well, gave me much, and promised still more. If he had only given me what he promised it would have been well for me. I could not get it because the King did not so wish. I was not the one who was remiss." [57] He then repeats the dating by the three King Henrys whom he had served and closes—forever —with these lines: "Here ends Wace's book; if anyone wishes to carry it forward let him do it." [58]

So far I have omitted all mention of argument over the date of Wace's birth. I think Gaston Paris' date of 1100, postulated on the poet's statement that he had heard his father mention the number of ships in the Conqueror's invading fleet, is too early. A twelfth-century man approaching seventy was good for very little, and Wace was active after 1170. Conditions of life in the twelfth century were much harder on the aged than they have been in the nineteenth and twentieth centuries. On the other hand, we must not rejuvenate Wace too much. The *Ricardus Wascii*, "Richard son of Wascius," who appears as a prebendary in Bayeux cathedral documents around 1200, could be a son

---

[56] *Rou*, III, 11,445 ff.: "Great shame does he do, there is none greater, who betrays his liege lord." The reference is to Henry I, who has betrayed Robert Courthose.

[57] *Rou*, III, 11,487–11,489.

[58] *Rou*, III, 11,501–11,502.

of Wace the chronicler. There is no evidence that Wace was not a married clerk, in lower orders.

In these pages I have sought to give an example of what I call "parallelism," an effort to outline the possibilities—the strong possibilities—that can be associated with the career of a medieval writer. When we limit ourselves only to those things that can be positively proved, the result is shallow indeed. On the other hand, too many critics make use of excessive generalization. Take, as an example, the assumption that Wace was a constant attendant at Henry II's court, merely because we know that he served under the three Henrys, and that the completed version of his *Brut* was presented to Eleanor of Aquitaine. We hope that these few pages have given a more balanced series of suppositions about Wace. This procedure might be tried with profit for many notable poets of the twelfth and thirteenth centuries.

IV

ETHICAL CRITICISM AND MEDIEVAL LITERATURE
Le roman de Tristan

Stephen G. Nichols, Jr.

*A*S LONG AS man has sought to express his vision of life in poetry, his perception has been judged by means of reference to the real world. Rightly or wrongly, there has always been a close parallelism between literature and society. What we expect from poetry, however, changes from age to age. Some ages have demanded little more from literature than entertainment; the nineteenth century rejected the French symbolist poets because their perception of the function of literature in relation to society differed so radically from that society's own view. In the belief prevailing at that time, literature was not meant to be "serious," at least not to the point of depicting life in terms of rotting corpses. Today, we demand more from literature; we look upon poetry as an instrument of knowledge about our lives. If the poetry of past ages is to retain its significance for us, it must be able to respond to the questions *we* ask of literature. The questions of the moment are largely existential: Why does man exist? For what purpose? What is his relationship to society as a whole? Of what use is the past?

When we ask such questions, we admit implicitly that the relation of literature to the society it reflects is central to the understanding of the actions, the behavior of the fictional beings.[1] For an observer, the character of a fictional being, like that of a real person, is the sum of his actions and words—the only means we have of knowing him. If we are to understand what he is and what he means to the central vision of the work, we must be able to achieve a meaningful interpretation of these actions and words. This interpretation must necessarily be made in terms of our own perspectives, but we must also be ready to take into account the ethical norms of the period in which the work was created.

The ethical norms of a period are of paramount importance if we are to understand the issues raised by a work in its time. We must never forget, however, that we are not dealing with the age itself, but rather with a work of art that has survived a bygone era. The norms of that age are important only in helping us to understand the work, to compare it with our own poetic expectations in order to grasp what there is in the work which makes us continue to accept it for itself, on its own terms, even though outwardly it may appear to represent an entirely different social and intellectual situation.

Some of the questions we seek to ask in such criticism are: Does the work reflect the intellectual preoccupations of its time? Or, on the contrary, does it seek to escape them? Is it fantasy? Does it mirror an ideal of the period? Does

---

[1] Paul Bénichou has expressed the parallelism of literature and society in the following words: "Rien ne contribue davantage à fortifier le sens du réel et du relatif, que le spectacle de la diversité ou des contradictions au sein des choses. C'est peu de distinguer une époque, un milieu, une ambiance sociale: il n'est pas d'époque qui ne soit le champ d'une lutte entre des idées contraires. Le rapport de la littérature et de la société n'est pas celui de deux êtres homogènes façonés à la ressemblance l'un de l'autre. La loi de la diversité et de la contradiction domine chacune d'elles et c'est de ce point de vue qu'on aperçoit le mieux leur dépendance réciproque. Les idées apparaissent d'autant plus liées à la société qu'on les conçoit davantage comme les éléments d'un débat qui accompagne et stimule les conflits réels de l'histoire" (*Morales du grand siècle* [Paris, 1948], p. 8).

it depict the morality of a particular class? Does its view of man complement or run counter to the views of the moment? [2] The discipline will remain literary so long as either the historical moment or the social milieu is not allowed to preempt attention to the point where it takes precedence over the work of art. Textual exegesis must precede historical evaluation; this is only logical, for we must first have a frame of reference to which the historical data can be related.

Let us turn to a work admirably suited to illustrate the working of ethical criticism: *Le roman de Tristan* by the medieval French poet, Béroul. In this work, as indeed with many of the medieval romances in which an adulterous relationship occupies a central and seemingly sympathetic position, it has long been a puzzle how the principal moral problem can be treated with such ambiguity. Ostensibly, the lovers contravene the most important political and religious institutions of twelfth-century France: feudalism and the Church. Instead of finding the combined authorities of these institutions united to punish the transgressions of Tristan and Iseut, we find, in the work, a pronounced effort to accommodate the affair, if not a complete apologia.

This feat is mainly accomplished by shifting the moral focus from the fact of the affair to its social setting. The genius of Béroul was to place the burden of perception onto the shoulders of those who would be responsible for dealing with it. The narrative does not recount the progress of the love affair as such, but rather the elusive and uncertain

---

[2] That such questions may help to discover previously unsuspected aspects of an author has recently been demonstrated by Pierre Jonin, "Aspects de la vie sociale au XIIe siècle dans *Yvain*" (*L'Information littéraire*, XVI [1964], 47–54). Jonin shows that the imaginary elements in *Yvain* are not so pervasive as had previously been thought. Chrétien relies on realistic detail, drawn from contemporary life, to reinforce his images.

confrontation of the affair by a society that is far from convinced that a guilty love exists between the two young people. The poet plays upon the ambiguity of action, the difficulty of interpreting even what we see with our own eyes, to create an atmosphere of equivocation favorable to the young couple. Béroul underscores the old psychological truth that perceived phenomena possess dual "realities": a reality independent of the beholder and the perceived "reality," that is, what he thinks he sees (which is frequently what he wants to see). Only someone outside the direct experiential range of the perceived phenomenon can tell whether the beholder's reality corresponds with the independent reality.

Béroul plays upon this phenomenon to create and maintain a tension between illusion and reality, making it extremely difficult for the other characters to judge the nature of Tristan's relations with Iseut. From the beginning, it is impossible for Mark to say with certainty that the couple is either guilty or innocent. Without such a determination, the affair cannot be subjected to universal moral laws. As long as a reasonable doubt as to the nature of the lovers' relationship remains, there is no official ground for condemnation. The poet is so careful to assure that there should be a reasonable doubt that he does not even include compromising scenes for the benefit of the audience. As for Mark, he never does knowingly witness a love scene. In the 4,500 lines left to us, the King has only one piece of concrete evidence that the lovers are intimate: the blood-flecked flour on the floor of the bedchamber. Even this evidence is circumstantial.

Before turning to examine the attitudes of the characters, let us briefly consider why the poet places so much importance on Mark's view of the affair; it is always through his eyes that the lovers are viewed at the crucial moments. In Mark, the personal and social victims of the transgression coalesce: he is at once outraged husband and betrayed *seigneur*. More important, it is he, in his role as Tristan's lord, who is responsible for dispensing justice. The affair must be proved to him before he can legally try the lovers.

The *roman* is naturally divided by the events into two parts. The first part consists of two major episodes: the two attempts to make Mark aware of the affair. It leads to a crisis, the denunciation and sentencing of the lovers. In the fragment as we have it, this crisis is the closest that Mark comes to confronting the fact of adultery. Instead of leading to a denouement and resolution, it leads to a suspension: the lovers flee society. Once outside the social order, the lovers are momentarily safe; they do not pose a direct threat to Mark's authority, nor can they be the focal point of the machinations of the evil barons. During this "truce," the author works out a formula that enables the lovers to rejoin society, to undergo the long-postponed judgment, and to be finally reinstated in the social milieu whose mores they seem to flaunt.

The fragment begins with Mark perched in a tree overlooking the trysting spot of the lovers. Before Tristan's arrival, Iseut discovers Mark's presence. Thanks to her quick wits and Tristan's sense of danger, they carry off the interview as though they were nothing more to each other than what their social and family roles proclaim them: nephew and aunt by marriage, and vassal and queen.

After they leave, Mark descends from the tree to ponder the meaning of the scene he has just witnessed. If the two are, as they appear, innocent, he has been forced, with the knowledge of one of his subjects (the dwarf, Frocin), to commit a humiliating and compromising act. Not only is his own royal dignity at stake, but also—since his behavior would accuse him of a lack of faith—the honor of his queen and that of a trusted vassal. Mark's actions are always circumscribed by the feudal relationship of seigneur and vassal. As soon as he recognizes before witnesses the possibility of felonious conduct on the part of one of his vassals, he is obliged to bring the matter before his feudal court for adjudication.[3] By failing to do so and, above all, by assuming the role of spy, he compromises his otherwise sound moral position.

Mark is incapable of facing the issue openly. As one of the characters later reports,

> Li rois n'a pas coraige entier
> Senpres est ci et senpres la.   (ll. 3432–3433)[4]

Rather than undertake a rational analysis of any situation, Mark prefers to let his imagination create hypothetical conclusions on which he then bases his decisions. The particularly high incidence of present and imperfect subjunctives in his speeches reveals the wild oscillations btween reality and illusion so typical of his emotional life.[5] His

---

[3] F. L. Ganshof reports the precise relations of vassal and lord in matters of feudal jurisdiction: "Powers of jurisdiction were . . . very closely bound up with feudal relationships. This was the case in particular with what one normally calls feudal jurisdiction, meaning by it cases arising out of the contract of vassalage and concerning its term or affecting the fief itself. This jurisdiction normally belonged to the lord, who exercised it over his vassals and over the fiefs held from him. . . . This power must have been acquired during the troubled and obscure years of the end of the ninth and the first third of the tenth century. Possibly the lord himself was at first the sole judge of failures or conflicts in the fields of vassal and feudal relationships, but from a quite early time, we find such disputes being decided by a court. . . . This court was presided over by the prince or the count, while his vassals assumed the duty of assessors. They probably united at an early date to allow cases which affected their relations with him or between themselves . . . to be submitted to the court in the same way as cases of a more strictly public character" (*Feudalism* [New York, 1961], pp. 158–159).

[4] All quotations are from *Le Roman de Tristan*, edited by Muret, revised by L. M. Defourques (4th ed.; Paris, 1962).

[5] Through free indirect discourse and direct discourse passages, we follow the tortuous paths of wish-oriented reasoning by which Mark—

unwillingness to face up to this emotional equivocation, to make the hard choice between reality and illusion, ultimately erodes any claim he might have to our sympathy and to his rights.

If Béroul is careful to put Mark's ethical position in jeopardy, he is just as careful to assure that the lovers will not be compromised. That they are lovers is clear from their own admission and the poet's, but we never see them engaged in conspicuous consumption, any more than does Mark. The most compromising scene in the whole work occurs on the night in which the dwarf arranges a trap by strewing the floor with flour, the idea being to record the footprints of anyone going from one bed to another in the royal chamber. Even here there is room for speculation as to whether the lovers do anything more than talk; certainly Mark does not catch them.

What is important for us to retain from the scene is that, for whatever purpose, the lovers were together, but seen only by Frocin, that shadowy personification of gratuitous hatred who wants to trap the lovers. By making the dwarf the only witness to so important a scene, Béroul

like his literary predecessors and successors, those cuckolded husbands who *will* themselves to blindness—tries to convince himself that illusion is reality, and reality, illusion. The key passage runs from line 295 to line 304. In it Mark begins by making a categorical statement of policy (to which he will not adhere) and then undertakes an analysis of the scene he has just witnessed. He alternates hypothesis with fact in a brilliant demonstration of false logic. He does not begin with a real fact, but with a hypothetical proposition, *S'il s'amasent de fol'amor* (l. 301). To this he appends an incontestable fact, *Ci avoient asez leisor* (l. 302), from which he draws the not necessarily logical conclusion *Bien les veïse entrebaisier* (l. 303), which is, in turn, shored up by another fact, *Ges ai oï si gramoier* (l. 304). Hypothesis, and fact are thus intercalated in *a b a b* order. By making the fact depend on a hypothesis, Mark arrives at the conclusion he subconsciously desires. Had he but reversed the order, he would have had perhaps a better chance of hitting upon the truth, or at least of recognizing there might have been more than one explanation for the lovers' behavior.

arranges for the picture to be obscured by the affective illusion-reality ambiguity characteristic of the very first scene. The ambiguity is strengthened by the fact that Tristan has regained his bed by the time the witnesses enter the room, leaving only the circumstantial evidence of the bloody sheets and the blood-flecked flour to mark his movement.

Even though the couple has not actually been caught *en flagrant délit,* there is strong evidence to indicate that they have been together, or at least to prove that Tristan has made an improper advance; but there is no evidence to prove the Queen's complicity. If the two were to be arraigned before a feudal court for proper trial and judgment, it would be difficult to believe that they could escape without some punitive sentence. In such a circumstance, the larger context of their relationship would have to be raised and the consequence faced.

The danger to the lovers is great, but Béroul averts the threat by a process similar to that already observed in the first scene. From the moment the threat arises, the emphasis shifts from the lovers and their indiscretion to the accusers and their behavior. The four barons who are the motivating force behind the attack on the lovers are shown to be consumed by jealousy because of the valorous deeds Tristan had previously performed, rather than moved by indignation at his moral laxity:

> Cuelli l'orent cil en haïne,
> Por sa prooise, et la roïne;
> Laidisent la, molt la menacent;
> Ne lairont justise n'en facent.   (ll. 773–776)

True, their motivation has no relevance to the legal question; but it does color the emotional atmosphere of the scene, and this climate in turn affects Mark's judgment. Because the barons hate Tristan so passionately, they have no difficulty in whipping up Mark's lacerated feelings to the point where he is able to think of nothing but vengeance.

In every sense, he transgresses the legal rights permitted an aggrieved husband under twelfth-century law. As Professor Pierre Jonin has so ably demonstrated, Mark proceeds as though he had caught the lovers *en flagrant délit*.[6] In doing so, he abbreviates shockingly the due process to which Tristan and the Queen are entitled. We have little difficulty in understanding how Mark's passions have been aroused until he believes he has taken the pair in flagrant delight, but the hard fact is that they have been taken in a situation where *flagrant délit* is only presumed.[7] Legally the distinction is quite important because in the latter instance Mark would not have the latitude in abrogating the legal procedure permitted in the former instance.

Not content with compromising the King legally, Béroul pushes him even further. As a punishment for their transgressions, Mark condemns the couple to the stake. In so doing, he exceeds absolutely the legal bounds laid down for such cases. No law authorizing so irrevocable a penalty has been discovered in the legal records of twelfth-century France. On the contrary, the laws seem to have been constructed with provision for repentance.[8] This opportunity

[6] "C'est la prise en flagrant délit et Marc déclare au coupable qu'il n'admet pas une justification qui serait sans valeur à ses yeux. Il lui annonce même qu'il pense le faire condamner à mort et exécuter le lendemain. ... Or le flagrant délit donne *ipso facto* au plaignant le droit de hâter la procédure au maximum. Tous les critiques sont d'accord à ce sujet" *Les Personnages féminins dans les romans français de Tristan au 12ᵉ siècle* [Gap, 1958], pp. 61–62).

[7] Rita Lejeune, in a long review article on Professor Jonin's book, makes the same observation: "Les tâches de sang sur la farine ne constituent pas, à bien y réfléchir, un véritable 'flagrant délit d'adultère' mais bien une présomption de flagrant délit" ("Les 'influences contemporaines' dans les romans français de Tristan au 12ᵉ siècle," *Le Moyen Âge*, LXVI [1960], 147).

[8] "Nouns devons convenir que malgré la diversité des châtiments variant avec les coutumes, nous n'avons pas trouvé parmi eux la peine

of course is exactly what Mark's wrathful sentence would deny the young couple.

The brutality of the sentence is second only to the treatment the King accords the prisoners before sentencing. The barons are allowed to maltreat both Tristan and Iseut shamelessly. The King himself is implicated in the outrages, inasmuch as the barons are acting on his orders in taking and binding the pair. It is not only our twentieth-century sensibilities that are shocked by the treatment, but those of the poet and the townspeople, who act as a chorus and maintain a running commentary sympathetic to the lovers throughout the long scene. Mark violates his own basically just nature to the ultimate degree when he abandons Iseut to the lepers after Tristan's escape. What her life would be like as an overworked bawd to the preternaturally ardent lepers is evoked in the most horrifying terms by the chief leper himself, with a malevolence that shocks even the King's entourage.[9]

Before the close of the scene, Mark has even been compromised in his behavior toward his loyal vassals, notably Dinas, his seneschal, who try to point out his unethical behavior in condemning the couple without benefit of a trial. It is left to the anonymous chorus of townspeople to sum up how much Mark is working against the best interests of his kingdom by acting as the agent of every evil influence that comes to hand in order to wreak his private vengeance:

de feu, du moins pour punir l'adultère. Les sanctions ont d'ailleurs perdu beaucoup de leur violence primitive. Le *livre de jostice et de plet* se contente de livrer les coupables au roi les deux premières fois et de les exiler à la troisième" (Jonin, *Les Personnages féminins*, p. 67).

[9] The gratuitously intense hatred exhibited by the dwarf, the barons, and the leper are too emphatic to be accidental. The feeling is partly that any force that purposely creates disharmony must be unnatural. In large measure, the intensity of the evil evoked is used to discredit those who would seek to harm the lovers. It is no accident that God is habitually shown as coming to the aid of Tristan and Iseut.

Certes en asez poi de borse
En porront metre le gaain.   (ll. 1080–1081)

The condemnation and flight of Tristan and Iseut are
an admission that their love, as it has existed heretofore,
is not stronger than the social order that was, in so many
ways, responsible for it. Faced with an open conflict between the contradictory roles, the lovers must choose the
one and relinquish the other. In this instance they are
forced to flee their social milieu. This does not imply a
moral condemnation—the author sedulously avoids the
broad question of morality—but implies rather the ex-
orcising of a weak point in the life of the kingdom. This
weakness is not in the lovers themselves, but in the attrac-
tion they hold for all the evil elements in the realm. They
provide a target for the sowers of discord. Chaos and disharmony combine to institute a reign of fear, hate, greed,
jealousy, and cowardice. Even the once-valiant Mark
succumbs to the baser emotions. The whole kingdom has
become tainted with the venom of the evil barons.

Although the lovers are ostensibly cut off from society
during their forest exile, it is not their private lives and
loves that are at the center of attention during the forest
interlude, but the society itself, in one form or another.
True, we are told that Tristan and Iseut, thanks to their
love, are able to endure the incredible deprivations of their
life in the forest (e.g., ll. 1365–1366, 1784–1786), but of
the six main scenes that constitute the episode, not one is
solely concerned with analyzing the love they share, nor
with recounting how they share it. This omission does not
mean that Béroul is incapable of describing their forest
life. Details of their daily life abound. We know how Tristan finds shelter for Iseut and himself in leafy bowers; how
he feeds the two of them on venison; how they are forced
to keep moving. These details give the narrative continuity
and serve as a constant comparison with the former life of
luxury they have been forced to abandon. In every sense,

the life they led in society continually obtrudes itself on
their life in the forest. Husdent, Tristan's hound, breaks
away to find his master; other characters search through
the forest. Finally Mark himself penetrates to the place
where the lovers lie sleeping. In an episode occupying more
than two hundred lines, the lovers themselves figure only
passively as the objects, first of Mark's hatred, then of his
compassion. In every sense, the narrative emphasis during
the forest interlude is on the bonds that link the lovers to
society, rather than on the love that separates them from
it. For example, the vivid images of physical suffering en-
dured by the couple,

> Molt les avra amors pené:
> Trois anz plainiers sofrirent peine,
> Lor char pali et devint vaine,   (ll. 2130–2132)

suggest that they are to be seen as undergoing a kind of
expiation and chastening, psychological as well as physical,
which can be the basis for a reconciliation with society. A
reconciliation is no longer merely a remote possibility, after
Mark's profession of compassion for the couple he finds
sleeping so chastely, drawn sword between them:

> Je lor ferai tel demostrance
> Que, ainçois qu'il s'esvelleront,
> Certainement savoir porront
> Qu'il furent endormi trové
> Et q'en a eü d'eus pité,
> Que je nes vuel noient ocire,
> Ne moi ne gent de mon enpire.   (ll. 2020–2026)

Certainly there can be no return to society if they are
merely to pick up where they left off, both living in the
household of the King and meeting secretly. There must
be a reorientation of their love to permit a more lasting
social accord. Above all, the fact of the affair must be
openly confronted. Without the rumor being confirmed or
denied once for all, the same syndrome of nasty hints and
spying will resume. If the couple were given the legal

sanction of trial and acquittal, it would become a felony for the evil barons to continue their insinuations.

The expected reorientation of the affair is prepared by two events. The first is the waning of the *amour-passion*, heralded by the expiration of the magic love-potion supposed to have been responsible for drawing them together in the first place. The fact that the first, passionate stage of their love matures to a more reasoned understanding in no way affects the reality of the love. It is as vital a force in the second part of the work as it is in the first. The maturer love does permit the lovers to think in terms of an accommodation with social realities, even to the point of living apart, if necessary, and seeing each other less frequently.

This psychological precondition allows the couple to take steps to effect a reentry into society; they begin by seeking a reconciliation with the Church. Heretofore, their passion has precluded any thought of repentance, without which there could be no hope of assistance from that powerful institution. With their passion controlled, an accommodation with the Church, for which true repentance is more important than past transgressions, can be worked out.

At the beginning of their forest sojourn, the lovers, seeking shelter, had visited the hermit Ogrin, a solitary monk. He had preached repentance to them on the grounds of strict Pauline thought. Without true repentance, he had said, they were as men dead:

> Et quel confort
> Puet on donner a home mort?
> Assez est mort qui longuement
> Gist en pechié, s'il ne repent.
> Doner ne puet nus penitance
> A pecheor sanz repentance.   (ll. 1387–1392)

Later on, when the lovers do finally return to submit themselves to the guidance of Ogrin, he figures as a much less doctrinaire spokesman for the Church. He accepts without question their professions, in which, to the objective, if not cynical, eye, no trace of repentance for past sins can be discerned in the words pronounced. Ogrin covers himself by not actually stating that their confession constitutes sufficient witness to their true repentance. Rather neglecting the religious aspect of the question, he busies himself on the practical side of the matter, counseling a less-than-honest version of their conduct as the basis for their reconciliation with Mark,

> Por honte oster et mal covrir
> Doit on un poi par bel mentir. (ll. 2353–2354)[10]

Ogrin is clearly somewhat less than orthodox as a cleric, but it would be overhasty to term him cynical, nor could his conduct be said to compromise the Church. Looking forward to the positive gains, he arranges for the return of a wife to her husband, a queen to her realm, and a discordant land to a harmonious state. He in no way sanctions the adultery, but recognizes that the possibility of a true repentance would be more likely within the social context than in the depths of the forest. Ogrin, like the poet him-

---

[10] At no time do we find the repentance demanded earlier. Tristan, in his statement to Ogrin, places the question in a purely social context. He recognizes the necessity for separation. Iseut is more alert to the moral question, but specifically rejects the idea of repenting her love for Tristan. She does say that henceforth they are freed from sharing their bodies, but the assertion is so phrased that it could be interpreted as meaning simply that because the potion has lapsed they are no longer forced to go on loving each other. This does not mean that they will not do so.

> Qar ja corage de folie
> Nen avrai je jor de ma vie.
> Ge ne di pas, a vostre entente,
> Que de Tristran jor me repente,
> Que je ne l'aim de bone amor
> Et com amis, sanz desanor:
> De la commune de mon cors
> Et je du suen somes tuit fors.   (ll. 2323–2330)

self, sees little to be gained by insisting on the universality of the moral question.

Once back in society, the lovers do give proof of their reorientation by the maturity of their conduct. They no longer look upon themselves as isolated in their own little world, but are able to understand that if they are to preserve the essence of their love, they must accept their separate roles as well. This new understanding is nowhere more evident than in the long scene of preparation for the ambiguous oath Iseut swears before the assembled courts of Arthur and Mark. Iseut's trial, in which she is to face and answer the charges brought by the barons, is the confrontation so long postponed.

Tristan is present at the ceremony and during the events preceding the oath. He is not there in his own raiment, but on the command of Iseut, disguised as a leper. Only Iseut and Dinas recognize him. The scene is reminiscent of the very first one because, once again, only the lovers have the key to the roles being played, while everyone else takes the illusion for the reality. The lovers themselves play their roles zestfully, fully aware of the humorous aspects of the *double entendre* they are acting out. Iseut even hints playfully that Tristan is not the penniless begger he seems when Tristan has the temerity to beg of Iseut herself:

> Par cele foi que je vos doi,
> Forz truanz est, asez en a,
> Ne mangera hui ce qu'il a.
> Soz sa chape senti sa guige.
> Rois, s'aloiere n'apetiche:
> Les pains demiés et les entiers
> Et les pieces et les quartiers
> Ai bien parmi le sac sentu.
> Viande a, si est bien vestu.
> De vos sorchauz, s'il les veut vendre,
> Puet il cinc soz d'esterlins prendre,
> Et de l'aumuce mon seignor.

Achat bien lit, si soit pastor,
Ou un asne qui past le tai.
Il est herlot, si que je sai.
Hui a suï bone pasture,
Trové a gent a sa mesure.
De moi n'en portera qui valle
Un sol ferlinc n'une maalle.   (ll. 3962–3980)

Henceforth, the interviews between the lovers will have to occur under similarly ambiguous conditions, themselves alone aware of the truth, while society contents itself with the image they allow it.[11]

From our analysis of Béroul's attitude toward the central moral problem posed by the legend of Tristan and Iseut, it appears that the poet has oriented the story toward the social question, rather than toward the love theme per se. Without sacrificing the fact of their love, he yet seeks to assure that the discordant elements of the story will be peacefully resolved. Unlike Marie de France, for example, Béroul does not shun the conflicts and contradictions of the real world of the twelfth century. Nor, like Chrétien de Troyes, does he plunge us exclusively into the world of a social class, the ruling aristocracy. Though the principal characters in Béroul's *roman* are indeed aristocrats, the people occupy a certain place in the general scene. They are not mute witnesses, but are used as a chorus in the "crowd" scenes. Through them we can assess the ethical attitudes of a class other than the ruling one toward the main events. For the people, Tristan is not merely a distant figure seen only on feast days parading to the lists. He is their champion, one to whom they owe the

[11] This seems to be one of the meanings of the two versions of the *Folie Tristan*, where Tristan, disguised once again, enters boldly into Mark's court. In the guise of a madman, he is able to converse freely about his love for Iseut. The reality thus improbably exposed, passes for the delusion of a madman, since it would be impossible for Iseut to love a bedunged maniac. Ironically, Tristan has no easy time, in the *Folie d'Oxford*, convincing Iseut herself that he really is Tristan, her lover.

lives of their children and the well-being and prosperity
of the country:

> Pleurent li grant e li petit,
> Sovent l'un d'eus a l'autre dit:
> "A! las, tant avon a plorer!
> Ahi! Tristan, tant par es ber!
> Qel damage qu'en traïson
> Vos ont fait prendre cil gloton!
> Ha! roïne franche, honoree,
> En qel terre sera mais nee
> Fille de roi qui ton cors valle?
> Ha! nains, ç'a fait ta devinalle!
> Ja ne voie Deu en la face,
> Qui trovera le nain en place,
> Qui nu ferra d'un glaive el cors!
> Ahi! Tristan, si grant dolors
> Sera de vos, beaus chiers amis,
> Qant si seroiz a destroit mis!
> Ha! las, quel duel de vostre mort!
> Qant le Morhout prist ja ci port,
> Qui ça venoit por nos enfanz,
> Nos barons fist si tost taisanz
> Que onques n'ot un si hardi
> Qui s'en osast armer vers lui.
> Vos enpreïstes la batalle
> Por nos trestoz de Cornoualle
> Et oceïstes le Morhout.
> Il vos navra d'un javelot,
> Sire, dont tu deüs morir.
> Ja ne devrion consentir
> Que vostre cors fust ci destruit."   (ll. 831–859)

Eschewing purely moral values, the people judge only the
social and personal worth of the Queen and Tristan, that is,
what the two have meant to them. In their eyes, the evil
clearly lies with those who would, for whatever reason,
attempt to deprive the realm of its vital human resources.

The attitude of the people corresponds to the expressed
sympathies of the poet himself, and of Mark, on more than

one occasion (e.g., ll. 3063–3079). Even the barons, themselves responsible for the persecution of the lovers, do not base their brief on moral grounds; the cankerous thought of Tristan's prowess and the acclaim he has won gnaw at them. If they attack him through his weakness, it is merely a matter of expediency, not morality.

How far can we label the attitudes expressed by Béroul and his characters as representative of twelfth-century feeling toward the difficult social and moral problem of adultery? Obviously, there can be no single answer, but we can examine the laws by which such transgressions were judged. These will provide some clue to contemporary moral attitudes insofar as they were reflected in the law.

Judging by the punishments prescribed for adultery, the juridical view varied from the rather lenient, as when a fine was levied, to the rather severe, as evidenced by a judgment of seven years' exile for repeated offenses.[12] In general, the punishment was harsher for men than for women. There were crimes held in far stronger legal, and presumably moral, disapprobation than adultery. Death by burning was regularly demanded for heretics, sodomites, serfs convicted of rising against their masters, and sometimes for rebels.[13]

If Béroul accurately reflects twelfth-century views regarding adultery, he also relies on a number of other contemporary attitudes. Pierre Jonin has made exhaustive studies of contemporary documents regarding jurisprudence, the degree of latitude permitted in manipulating justificatory oaths, the status and treatment of banished persons, and so on. For every sociolegal procedure utilized by Béroul, except the punishment proposed by Mark, which was purposefully harsh as we saw, Professor Jonin finds a corresponding historical reality:

[12] Jonin, *Les Personnages féminins*, pp. 66–70.
[13] *Ibid.*, p. 70.

Sur ce procès et l'attitude d'Iseut au cours de ses étapes, il est maintenant possible de porter un jugement. A une exception près, le châtiment proposé pour l'adultère, il n'est aucune de ces phases qui ne s'explique par les coutumiers contemporaines. Toutes les mesures prises y trouvent leur justification. ... Dans l'ensemble de cette poursuite judiciaire, épisode aussi long qu'important dans Béroul, Iseut reste assujettie à la juridiction médiévale, victime ou bénéficière.[14]

On the other hand, Béroul's attempts to place the reoriented affair under the aegis of the Church seems not to reflect with any degree of fidelity even the most liberal elements of the contemporary religious movements. While there is no doubt that many a chaplain in aristocratic circles was often called upon to put a good front on the peccadilloes of his flock (and even to baptize some of them), one finds no record of religious doctrines allowing white lies to be substituted for true repentance. Certain laxist theologians did, it is true, admit instances where fraudulent statements could be justified. Among these men is St. Hilary, the saint Iseut swears by at her trial, although the examples of mitigating circumstances which he gives do not specifically cover Iseut's situation.[15] What Béroul has done is to fuse, in the person of Ogrin, a number of laxist tendencies current in liberal (or corrupt) religious circles and carry them one step further to cover the difficult material of his story. Ogrin does not condone the adultery, but rather creates a milieu that could foster a true repentance. There is no doubt, however, that the ethical norms reflected are secular, rather than religious; they show us in what ways the modalities of the secular and religious norms were contradictory.

[14] *Ibid.*, pp. 108–109. In her review, Mme Lejeune (*op. cit.*), not an easy critic, nevertheless finds Jonin's study to be a useful contribution with which many of her own independent studies are in accord.

[15] Jonin, *Les Personnages féminins*, p. 346; see also Lejeune, *op. cit.*, pp. 156–159.

Let us not forget that Béroul was not alone in projecting secular needs into a religious context. During his lifetime, the Church was in the throes of the Gregorian Reform; simony and clerical marriages were two of the most hotly contested practices. The latter, especially, raised the specter of physical love in the bosom of the Church itself. The records are not wanting in stories of men who held high offices in the Church, while at the same time ruling dukedoms, begetting heirs by legitimate wives, and maintaining mistresses.[16] On an even larger scale, the whole system of the medieval Church has been likened to a machine not unlike the secular political variety. As R. W. Southern has observed, the system "was, as practical men knew, capable of being manipulated. . . . The whole secret lay in knowing the ropes, and in sensing how far one could go." [17]

It would be a mistake to think that the realistic detail of Béroul's *roman* was an end in itself; he is not a realist *avant la lettre*. On the contrary, his interest lies with the human and social tragedy inherent in the love triangle in which a legendary destiny has enmeshed the three principals. In attempting to accommodate the ancient legend to an authentic twelfth-century setting, Béroul emphasizes that part of the problem which seems most germane to a time and a country that went further than any other in elaborating a code for extraconjugal love. Pragmatist to the core, though not without a certain idealism, Béroul asks if it is possible for a love such as that of Tristan and Iseut to exist without threatening the social harmony of the kingdom.

[16] C. N. L. Brooke, "Clerical Marriage in England, 1050–1200" (in *Change in Medieval Society,* ed. Sylvia Thrupp [New York, 1964], pp. 49–63, esp. p. 62), gives an excellent study of the practice and ultimate decline of clerical marriage and its abuses. His study reveals graphically how an officially condemned practice could flourish so long as it was not considered immoral by society. From the date when the moral question of clerical marriage penetrated into the social order, the practice began to disappear.

[17] *The Making of the Middle Ages* (New Haven, 1961), p. 134.

In the surviving part of our fragment, the answer is "yes," provided the lovers are willing to make certain concessions to society, the chief one being to maintain before the public the illusion that their love is no love. That they are willing to do so indicates the extent of their commitment to life.

We must finally ask whether the desire to reconcile the discordant elements of the legend is in itself an authentic twelfth-century attitude. There can be little doubt that the desire to strive for a harmonious order was one of the strongest philosophical traditions in the Middle Ages. E. R. Curtius, in his earlier studies on medieval aesthetics and, later, in *European Literature and the Latin Middle Ages*, showed that a basic concern of patristic thought was to assimilate in one continuous, concordant system all learning, even the disparate bodies of classical letters. No matter how contradictory a classical author might appear to Christian doctrine, he could be, and was, fitted into the Christian world view.[18]

Taking his departure from a different point, Leo Spitzer observed the same tendency to seek harmony in discord, only he felt it to be a general Western ideal not limited solely to the Middle Ages, in which it had enjoyed, nevertheless, its most extensive vogue. In a work that occupied much of his later years, Spitzer traced the history of the *concordia discors* ideal.[19] He finds that no major medieval philosopher escaped the all-pervading ideal of world harmony. The vocabulary and themes of the early vernacular

[18] See especially "Zur Literarästhetik des Mittelalters," *Zeitschrift für romanische Philologie*, LVIII (1938), 433–479, specifically, 464–477.

[19] "The making concordant of the discordant" confronts us with two antagonistic forces of harmonious unification and discordant manifoldness, but the συμφρόνησις, the 'thinking together' is triumphant; the discordant is made subject thereto (the linguistic expression itself portrays the wrestling with chaos and the triumph of cosmos)" (*Classical and Christian Ideas of World Harmony*, ed. A. G. Hatcher [Baltimore, 1963], p. 9).

poets also abound in examples of the idea, but it was, of course, Dante who gave it its most magnificent literary expression.

That Béroul should have been motivated by such an ideal is not surprising. That he should have succeeded in this ideal as well as he did tells us much about the moral climate of his time. But, ultimately, we must conclude that the degree of his success in imposing a solution that is no solution, despite the strident note of realism in his work, is the margin between the world of art and reality.